111 Fried Rice Recipes

(111 Fried Rice Recipes - Volume 1)

Marie Chunn

Copyright: Published in the United States by Marie Chunn/ © MARIE CHUNN

Published on November, 24 2020

All rights reserved. No part of this publication may be reproduced, stored in retrieval system, copied in any form or by any means, electronic, mechanical, photocopying, recording or otherwise transmitted without written permission from the publisher. Please do not participate in or encourage piracy of this material in any way. You must not circulate this book in any format. MARIE CHUNN does not control or direct users' actions and is not responsible for the information or content shared, harm and/or actions of the book readers.

In accordance with the U.S. Copyright Act of 1976, the scanning, uploading and electronic sharing of any part of this book without the permission of the publisher constitute unlawful piracy and theft of the author's intellectual property. If you would like to use material from the book (other than just simply for reviewing the book), prior permission must be obtained by contacting the author at author@fetarecipes.com

Thank you for your support of the author's rights.

Content

111 AWESOME FRIED RICE RECIPES 5

1. 14 Th Ave Cafe Fried Rice Recipe 5
2. Almost Classic Pork Fried Rice Recipe 5
3. Anyday Fried Rice Recipe 6
4. Authentic Chinese Fried Rice Recipe 6
5. Bacon Fried Rice Recipe 7
6. Baked Fried Rice Recipe 7
7. Beef Fried Rice Recipe 7
8. Brown Fried Rice Thats Oh So Nice Recipe 8
9. Chicken And Veggie Fried Rice Recipe 8
10. Chicken Fried Rice Recipe 9
11. Chinease Style Rice Recipe 9
12. Chinese Fried Rice Recipe 9
13. Chinese Style Fried Rice Recipe 10
14. Coconut Fried Rice Recipe 10
15. Cuban Fried Rice Recipe 11
16. Curry Ginger Peppers With Rice Recipe .. 11
17. Day Old Fried Rice Recipe 12
18. Easy Chinese Fried Rice Recipe 12
19. Easy Fried Rice Recipe 13
20. Easy Indonesian Fried Rice Nasi Goreng Recipe 13
21. Egg Fried Rice Recipe 14
22. Egg Fried Rice With Chicken And Prawns Recipe 14
23. Elaines Chinese Fried Rice Recipe 15
24. Emelis Seafood Fried Rice Recipe 15
25. FRIED RICE AND PASTA Recipe 16
26. Fancy Pineapple Thai Fried Rice Recipe .. 16
27. Fast Fried Rice Recipe 17
28. Fast Veggie Stir Fry Recipe 17
29. Favorite Fried Rice Recipe 17
30. Fried Forbidden Rice Recipe 18
31. Fried Rice Noodle Recipe 18
32. Fried Rice Recipe 19
33. Fried Rice With Lobster Recipe 19
34. Fried Rice With Tofu Recipe 19
35. Fried Rice With Bacon Recipe 20
36. Garlic Fried Rice Recipe 20
37. Ginger Fried Rice Recipe 20
38. Ginger Fried Rice With Shitake Mushrooms Recipe 21
39. Golden Fried Rice Recipe 21
40. Hibachi Style Fried Rice Recipe 22
41. How To Make Egg Fried Rice Recipe 22
42. INDONESIAN FRIED RICE NASI GORENG Recipe 22
43. Improvised Thai Stir Fried Rice Recipe 23
44. Island Fried Rice Recipe 24
45. JDs Sardine Fried Rice Recipe 24
46. Laurie's Fried Rice Recipe 25
47. Leftover Ham Fried Rice Recipe 25
48. Mai Pen Rai Shrimp And Chicken Thai Fried Rice Recipe 25
49. Making Fabulous Fried Rice Recipe 26
50. Mango Pork Fried Rice Recipe 26
51. Mexican Fried Rice Recipe 27
52. Millies Fried Rice Recipe 27
53. Minced Beef Fried Rice Recipe 27
54. Moms Fried Rice Recipe 28
55. Multi Flavored Thai Fried Rice Recipe 28
56. Mushroom Fried Rice Recipe 29
57. Mushrooms And Anchovies Fried Rice Recipe 29
58. My Favorite Far East Fried Rice Recipe.... 30
59. Nasi Goreng Indonesian Fried Rice Recipe 30
60. Oven Fried Rice Recipe 31
61. PORK FRIED RICE Recipe 31
62. Paella Style Fried Rice Recipe 32
63. Papa Oning's "Sinalamog" Fried Rice Recipe 32
64. Pauls Chicken Fried Rice Recipe 32
65. Peruvian Fried Rice Recipe 33
66. Peruvian Style Fried Rice Recipe 33
67. Pinapple Shimp Fried Rice Recipe 34
68. Pineapple "fried" Rice Recipe 34
69. Pineapple Fried Rice Recipe 35
70. Pineapple Fried Rice Recipe 35
71. Pineapple Thai Fried Rice Recipe 35
72. Pork Fried Rice Recipe 36
73. Proper Fried Rice Takeaway Style Recipe. 36
74. Quick And Easy Fried Rice Recipe 37
75. Red Curry Fried Rice Recipe 37
76. Red Fried Rice Recipe 38
77. Rice And Corn Recipe 38
78. Salted Fish Rice Recipe 38
79. Sausage Or Spam Fried Rice Recipe 39
80. Sauteed Rice With Cumin Seeds Mustard

Seeds Onions Curry Leaves Green Chilli Coriander Turmeric Recipe 39
81. Scallop Fried Rice Recipe 40
82. Shiitake "Fried" Rice Recipe..................... 40
83. Shrimp Fried Rice Recipe 41
84. Simple Fried Rice Recipe 41
85. Simple Indian Fried Rice Recipe 41
86. Simple Yummy Fried Rice Recipe............ 42
87. Soy Free Chicken Fried Rice Recipe......... 42
88. Spanish Fried Rice Recipe 43
89. Spicy Chicken Fried Rice Recipe 43
90. Stir Fried Rice Recipe 44
91. Szechuan Orange Chicken Fried Rice Recipe 44
92. Tea Fried Rice Recipe.................................. 45
93. Thai Fried Rice Recipe 45
94. Thai Red Curry Fried Rice Recipe 45
95. Thai Shrimp Fried Rice With Pineapple Recipe 46
96. Tomato Fried Rice Recipe 46
97. Tuna Fried Rice Recipe 47
98. Vegetable Fried Rice Recipe....................... 47
99. Vegetarian Fried Rice Recipe 47
100. Vietnamese Fried Rice Recipe 48
101. Wild Rice Stir Fried Recipe 49
102. Yang Chow Fried Rice Recipe 49
103. Yangchow Fried Rice Recipe 50
104. Chinese Shrimp Fried Rice Recipe............. 50
105. Chinese Fried Rice Recipe 51
106. Korean Kimchi Fried Rice Recipe 51
107. Malaysian Fried Rice Recipe....................... 51
108. Quick Fried Rice Recipe 51
109. Shannons Fried Rice Recipe........................ 52
110. Thai Seafood And Pork Fried Rice Recipe 52
111. Thai Spicy Fried Rice Recipe 53

INDEX **54**

CONCLUSION **56**

111 Awesome Fried Rice Recipes

***

1. 14 Th Ave Cafe Fried Rice Recipe

Serving: 8 | Prep: | Cook: 15mins | Ready in:

Ingredients

- 3 Tbsp. vegetable oil
- 2 cloves garlic, minced (2 teaspoons)
- 1 rib celery, chopped
- 2 strips bacon, chopped
- 2 oz. cooked ham, chopped (1/3 cup)
- 2 eggs, lightly beaten
- 4 C. cooled cooked white rice (1-1/3 cups uncooked)
- 1/2 C. mixed frozen peas and carrots, thawed
- 3 Tbsp. reduced-sodium soy sauce
- 1 Tbsp. fish sauce (nam pla), available in Asian markets
- Pinch black pepper
- 1/4 C. chopped green onion

Direction

- Heat a large skillet or wok and add the oil. Add garlic, celery, and bacon and cook, stirring constantly, about 3 minutes. Add ham and eggs; cook, stirring, until lightly browned. Add rice, peas and carrots; toss well to mix thoroughly. Add soy and fish sauces and pepper; stir-fry about 5 minutes. Add green onions; cook, stirring constantly, about 3 minutes longer or until done.

2. Almost Classic Pork Fried Rice Recipe

Serving: 4 | Prep: | Cook: 25mins | Ready in:

Ingredients

- 2 TB peanut oil or olive oil
- 1/2 tsp kosher salt,divided
- 1/2 lb boneless pork loin chop,cut in 1/2" pieces
- 1/2 c chopped carrot
- 1/2 c chopped celery
- 1/2 c chopped green onion bottoms(white part)
- 2 TB minced garlic
- 2 TB minced,peeled,fresh ginger
- 3 c cooked ,chilled long-grain brown rice (or white,brown is healthier)
- 1 large egg
- 3 TB mirin or dry sherry
- 3 TB lower-sodium soy sauce
- 1 tsap dark sesame oil
- 1/4 tso fresh ground black pepper
- 2 c fresh bean sprouts
- 1/4 c cannes,diced water chestnuts,rinsed and drained
- 1 c chopped green onion tops

Direction

- Heat a large skillet over med-high heat. Add 1 TB peanut oil to pan, swirl to coat. Sprinkle 1/8 tsp salt over pork. Add pork to pan and sauté for 2 mins or till browned on all sides
- Remove pork from pan. Add carrot and celery to pan and sauté 2 mins or till lightly browned, stirring frequently. Add carrots mixture to pork.
- Add remaining 1 TB peanut oil to pan, swirling to coat. Stir in green onion bottoms, garlic and ginger; cook 15 seconds, stirring constantly. Add rice, stirring well to coat rice with oil; cook without stirring, for 2 mins or till edges begin to brown. Stir rice mixture

and cook without stirring, an additional 2 min or till edges begin to brown. Make a well in center of rice mixture.
- Add egg, stir-fry for 30 seconds or till soft-scrambled, stirring constantly.
- Return pork mixture to pan. Stir in mirin or sherry and cook 1 min or till mirin is absorbed. Stir in remaining 3/8 tsp salt, soy sauce, sesame oil and pepper. Remove from heat and stir in bean sprouts and water chestnuts.
- Sprinkle with green onion tops.

3. Anyday Fried Rice Recipe

Serving: 4 | Prep: | Cook: 5mins | Ready in:

Ingredients

- 1 tbspoon chopped garlic
- 1 small onion chopped
- 2 tbspoons butter or vegetable oil
- 4 cups of plain white left over rice (new cooked rice also ok)
- 1/2 cup of ready mixed frozen veggies
- 2 teaspoons fermented baby shrimps (bagoong alamang) or
- 1/2 teaspoon salt (use only if fermented shrimp is not available
- 1 pcs. regular hotdog or 2 slices of ham (cut into very small cubes)
- 1 medium beaten egg (optional)

Direction

- Heat butter or oil in frying pan over medium heat
- Add chopped garlic and onion in heated butter or oil, stir until slightly brown (if using butter, be sure not to burn butter)
- Add in mixed veggies, hotdog or ham pieces, stir fry 1 min.
- Add left over rice and stir fry for about 2 mins.
- Add fermented shrimp (salt if fermented shrimp is not available),
- Continue stirring until all ingredients are well mixed
- Add beaten egg to fried rice and cook for 1 min. (egg, optional)
- Place slices of luncheon meat on top before serving if desired
- Best serve when hot, serves 4

4. Authentic Chinese Fried Rice Recipe

Serving: 4 | Prep: | Cook: 10mins | Ready in:

Ingredients

- 12 oz. long-grain rice
- 3 pieces bacon
- 8 oz. Chinese barbecued pork tenderloin
- 1 cup cooked peas
- 3 eggs
- salt and pepper
- oil
- 2 tsp. grated green ginger
- 8 shallots or spring onions
- 1 lb. prawns
- 2 tbsp. oil, extra
- 2 tsp. soya sauce

Direction

- The day before:
- Make rice and spread evenly over two large cookie trays. Refrigerate overnight. Stir occasionally to allow rice to dry completely. If you want to serve rice the same day, spread out on shallow trays, put in moderate oven (325 F.) 15 to 20 minutes; stir rice every five minutes to bring the moist grains to the top.
- Finely dice bacon, fry until crisp, and drain; slice pork thinly. Beat eggs lightly with fork, season with salt and pepper. Heat a small quantity of oil in pan, pour in enough of egg mixture to make one pancake; turn; cook other side. Remove from pan, repeat with remaining egg mixture. Roll up pancakes, slice into thin

strips. Finely chop shallots, shell and devein prawns, if large cut into smaller pieces. Heat extra oil in pan or wok. Sauté ginger one minute, stir in rice, stir five minutes. Add bacon, pork, shallots, peas, egg strips and prawns, mix lightly. When completely heated add soya sauce, mix well.

5. Bacon Fried Rice Recipe

Serving: 6 | Prep: | Cook: 15mins | Ready in:

Ingredients

- 4 cups cooked white rice(can sub brown for a different texture, flavor), cooled(leftover is fine!)
- about 1t rice vinegar
- 1/2lb bacon, chopped
- 1/4-1t red pepper flakes and or a healthy dash of hot chili sauce
- dash(and I mean a DASH) of sesame oil(optional)
- 2 eggs, slightly beaten
- 3-4 green onions
- couple t soy sauce or teriyaki sauce(I greatly dislike teriyaki, and can barely stand soy alone, so I use a sauce called Dale's. It's about all I can handle :)
- fresh ground pepper blend, or black pepper

Direction

- Add vinegar to rice and toss well . Set aside.
- In medium skillet or wok (I like the texture and flavor that cast iron brings, so I use it) brown bacon pieces until done.
- Set bacon aside but leave grease.
- Add red pepper flakes and rice to pan and cook over medium heat, stirring frequently, so make sure every grain gets covered with the fat.
- Add beaten eggs and immediately stir quickly to not get big lumps of scrambled egg. :) You are just looking for the lil bits to run throughout the rice.
- Continue to stir and toss well and add bacon, soy sauce, sesame oil, green onions and pepper.
- Cook until just warmed through.
- *PLEASE NOTE* this rice doesn't taste like bacon, exactly, but the bacon, does...errr...obviously. ;) The point is, if you just want a flavorful fried rice but not to have bits of bacon, simply fry half a pound of bacon, remove it and save it or use it for breakfast the next morning, and continue with the recipe, not adding the bacon back in. You'll still get a wonderful, different variation of a classic dish. :)

6. Baked Fried Rice Recipe

Serving: 8 | Prep: | Cook: 75mins | Ready in:

Ingredients

- 1/2 pkg onion soup mix
- 1/2 can mushrooms
- 1 c rice (I use converted white rice for this)
- 1/4 c soya sauce
- 1/8 c oil
- 1 3/4 c water

Direction

- Bake covered at 350 degrees for 1 hr. 15 minutes
- The original recipe is doubled and should bake for 1 hr. 45 minutes

7. Beef Fried Rice Recipe

Serving: 4 | Prep: | Cook: 25mins | Ready in:

Ingredients

- 3 cups of cooked rice
- 3 tbsp. of oil
- 3 glove garlic crushed
- pinch of black pepper
- 3 tbsp. fish sauce or to taste
- pinch of msg (optional)
- 1 cup of beef tenderion thinly sliced
- 1/2 cup of green onion long sliced
- 2 tbsp. thick soy sauce (optional)
- 1/2 onion medium size sliced

Direction

- In a wok or skillet, add oil and garlic cook until golden brown.
- Add beef, cook roughly until done.
- Add onion and cook for another 2-3 minutes
- Add rice, fish sauce, thick soy sauce, msg and black pepper. Mix well
- Add green onion and stir to coat and it ready to serve
- Best serve hot!!!

8. Brown Fried Rice Thats Oh So Nice Recipe

Serving: 24 | Prep: | Cook: 5mins | Ready in:

Ingredients

- 1.5 Cups brown rice
- 2 jumbo eggs
- 1 Large green onion, chopped
- 1 block firm tofu
- 4 apple-Chicken sausage links (Aidell's Brand)
- 3/4 Cup soy sauce
- 1/4 Cup olive oil

Direction

- *NOTE RICE SHOULD BE COOKED BEFORE INITIAL PREP, PREFERABLY HAVING BEEN IN A FREEZER TO MAKE RICE FIRM*
- Take two jumbo eggs, scramble then cook. Set aside.
- Chop a large stalk of green onions. Set aside.
- Cut firm tofu block into small cubes. Set aside.
- Take Aidell's Apple-Chicken Sausage and cut into small pieces. Set aside.
- Heat large skillet (preferably Wok skillet), and add 1/4 cup of olive oil.
- Add green onions to skillet.
- Stir tofu into skillet.
- Stir Rice into skillet.
- Stir scrambled eggs into skillet.
- Stir in Apple-Chicken Sausage.
- Slowly pour in 3/4 cup of soy sauce.
- Stir all ingredients until complete.
- Serve warm.

9. Chicken And Veggie Fried Rice Recipe

Serving: 8 | Prep: | Cook: 25mins | Ready in:

Ingredients

- 1 cup rice 2 cups water, plus salt
- 1 chicken breast, approx. 1 cup cut into 1/2 inch pieces
- 1 stalk celery, sliced
- 4 oz. mushrooms, roughly chopped
- 3 eggs, beaten
- 1/4 cup low sodium soy sauce, I use Bragg's
- 3 Tbs avocado oil, or more
- 1 cup frozen peas, thawed and warmed
- 3-4 green onions, sliced

Direction

- Cook the rice in salted water, the day before is best
- Heat 1 Tbsp. of oil in a wide bottom frying pan.
- Add the chicken and cook until no longer pink, approx. 5 mins.
- Remove chicken to a warm bowl.
- Add 2 Tbsp. of oil to the pan, high heat.

- Add the mushrooms and celery and cook for approx. 5 mins or until celery is slightly soft.
- Push the veggies to the side of the pan.
- Tilt the pan 90 degrees and add the eggs. Cook for about 3 mins, scrambling.
- Mix eggs and veggies together.
- Add the rice to the pan and stir for about 2 mins.
- Add the chicken
- Add the soy sauce and stir well.
- Add the green onions and peas and stir
- Serve and enjoy!!

10. Chicken Fried Rice Recipe

Serving: 6 | Prep: | Cook: 20mins | Ready in:

Ingredients

- 1 T. toasted sesame oil or cooking oil
- 2 beaten eggs
- 2 T. cooking oil
- 3 cloves garlic, minced
- 8 oz. whole mushrooms, large ones quartered, medium ones cut in half, small ones leave whole (mushrooms shrink when cooked, keep them big enough so they don't disappear into the rice)
- 1 cup julienne/matchstick carrots
- 1 cup peas
- 9-12 T. reduced-sodium soy sauce
- 6-9 T. sherry
- Dash cayenne pepper
- 3 cups (before cooking) instant rice, cooked & chilled
- 3 chicken breasts, cooked & shredded
- 3 thinly sliced green onions

Direction

- In a large skillet, heat the sesame oil over medium heat. Tilt pan to completely cover bottom of pan with oil. Add eggs, lifting and tilting the skillet to form a thin layer. Cook for 1 minute or until egg is set. Invert skillet over a cutting board to remove cooked egg. Cut egg into short narrow strips. Set aside.
- In the same skillet, cook and stir 2 T. oil, garlic, mushrooms and carrots about 5 minutes, or until mushrooms are as done as you like them.
- Add peas to skillet. Cook until crisp-tender, just a minute or two.
- Stir in 9 T. soy sauce, 6 T. wine and cayenne pepper.
- Add egg strips, cooked rice, cooked chicken and green onions. Stir to combine. If mixture looks too dry, or you like more sauce, add more soy sauce, wine and cayenne pepper to taste. Cook and stir until mixture is heated thru, about 5-10 minutes.

11. Chinease Style Rice Recipe

Serving: 0 | Prep: | Cook: | Ready in:

Ingredients

- 1 1/4 c water
- 1 egg
- 1/3 c chopped onion
- 1 1/2 c quick rice
- 3 tbsp butter
- 2-3 tsp soy sauce

Direction

- Stir rice into boiling water cover and remove from heat let stand for 5 minutes. In a 10 inch skillet cook slightly beaten egg in butter add onion and rice. Sauté stirring over medium heat until mixture is lightly browned. Mix soy sauce with 3/4 c water and stir into rice cook until browned.

12. Chinese Fried Rice Recipe

Serving: 5 | Prep: | Cook: 20mins | Ready in:

Ingredients

- 1 1/2 cups of rice
- 2 Medium sized mushrooms
- 1/2 capsicum
- 1/2 stalk of shallots
- 1/2 cup of snow peas
- 1/2 onion
- 1/2 cup of corn
- 1/2 cup of mint peas
- 1 cup of mixted vegetables (frozen)
- 1 chicken thigh
- 1/2 cup of sliced ham

Direction

- Set oven temperature to 100 degrees C.
- Boil some water on the stove. When boiled, add the rice along with 1/2 teaspoon of oil and a teaspoon of salt, boiling for 12 minutes, stirring 3-4 times.
- When cooked drain the water out of the rice but DO NOT rinse with water. Spoon rice onto a tray and put in oven.
- Slice chicken into small pieces and stir-fry in a wok. Remove chicken and put aside.
- Cut up remaining ingredients and stir-fry in the wok. When cooked add chicken and continue to stir-fry.
- Once cooked to satisfy add rice and mix ingredients all together. Add some soy sauce and then serve into bowls.
- Add soy sauce to taste and enjoy your quick, easy and healthy meal!

13. Chinese Style Fried Rice Recipe

Serving: 4 | Prep: | Cook: 40mins | Ready in:

Ingredients

- 2 cups uncooked basmati rice
- 2 cups water
- 1/2 cup ham steak (cut into cubes:pea size)
- 1/2 cup frozen peas & carrots
- 1 cup thinly sliced green onion
- 1/3 cup chopped shiitake mushroom
- 3 eggs, lightly beaten
- 3-4 tablespoons canola oil (or peanut oil)
- 1/4 teaspoon salt
- 1/4 tsp white pepper
- 1 Tbsp oyster sauce
- 1 tsp sugar

Direction

- Cook your rice (I use a rice cooker). You want it a bit on the crunchy side, so even though you might want to add more water, DON'T.
- Let your rice cool completely (I spread it out on a baking sheet and put it in the freezer if I'm in a hurry). You can even cook your rice the night before and let cool in the fridge.
- In wok or heavy large sauté pan over moderately high heat, heat oil until hot but not smoking. Add half of scallions (reserve remainder for garnish) about 1-2 minutes.
- Add eggs and rice and stir-fry until eggs are just set, about 1 minute. Add mushrooms, peas, ham, oyster sauce, sugar, salt, and pepper and stir-fry until heated through and fluffy, 4 to 5 minutes.
- Garnish with remaining scallions and serve.

14. Coconut Fried Rice Recipe

Serving: 4 | Prep: | Cook: 25mins | Ready in:

Ingredients

- 2 large eggs (use higher omega-3 fatty acid eggs if available)
- 1/4 cup egg substitute
- Canola cooking spray
- 1 tablespoon canola oil
- 1 sweet or yellow onion, finely chopped
- 2 to 3 teaspoons minced garlic (depending on your preference)
- 1/2 teaspoon salt (optional)
- 1/2 teaspoon black pepper

- 2 tablespoon catsup
- 1 cup finely diced tomato
- 1/4 cup low-fat milk (or substitute whole milk or fat-free half-and-half)
- A pinch or two of saffron (available in small jars in the spice section of your market)
- A pinch or two of curry powder
- 1/4 teaspoon coconut extract
- 4 cups cooked brown rice (use a rice cooker, or cook on the stove)
- 8 ounces or more frozen, cooked, shelled and de-veined shrimp, thawed; diced tofu; or cooked and shredded or diced chicken, beef, or pork (optional)
- 1/2 cup chopped green onions
- 1/4 cup chopped fresh cilantro leaves

Direction

- 1. Add eggs and egg substitute to medium bowl and beat with fork until well blended. Coat a large, non-stick wok or frying pan with canola cooking spray and start heating over medium-high heat. Pour in the egg mixture and either scramble or cook like an omelet (your choice). Set cooked eggs aside. If you made an omelet, cut into shreds before setting aside.
- 2. To the same wok or frying pan, add canola oil and heat over medium-high heat. Add onions and garlic and stir-fry until golden (a few minutes). Add salt (if desired), pepper, catsup, and diced tomato, and continue to stir-fry for a minute or two. Meanwhile, add the milk, saffron, curry and coconut extract to a 1-cup measure and stir to blend.
- 3. Add the brown rice, shrimp and coconut milk mixture to the wok with the onion mixture and continue to stir-fry for a couple more minutes. Stir in the cooked egg pieces or strips.
- 4. Arrange each serving of rice in a bowl and garnish with green onions and cilantro.

15. Cuban Fried Rice Recipe

Serving: 4 | Prep: | Cook: 20mins | Ready in:

Ingredients

- 1 small fresh pineapple, peeled, and cored, cut in a container reserve any pinapple liquid
- 1 Tbsp. olive oil
- 2 cups cooked long grain rice
- 12 oz. cooked ham, coarsely chopped
- 1 cup chopped or sliced sweet peppers
- 1 jalapeño pepper, sliced
- 1/2 15-oz. can black beans, rinsed and drained (3/4 cup)
- lime wedges

Direction

- Cut pineapple in 3/4-inch slices.
- Heat oil in 12-inch skillet over medium-high heat; add pineapple slices.
- Cook 3 to 4 minutes or until beginning to brown.
- Divide pineapple among four plates.
- Meanwhile, prepare rice according to package directions to make 2 cups
- Add ham and peppers to skillet; cook 3 minutes, stirring occasionally.
- Add beans and rice.
- Cook, stirring occasionally, 3 minutes or until heated through.
- Stir in reserved pineapple juice if there is any
- Serve with lime wedges.

16. Curry Ginger Peppers With Rice Recipe

Serving: 0 | Prep: | Cook: 30mins | Ready in:

Ingredients

- brown rice (1 cup uncooked) - I made this as I was cooking, but I know its better to use cold rice.

- 3 green onions
- 1 red bell pepper
- 2 cloves garlic
- 1-2 carrots
- curry powder
- ginger
- sesame seeds
- sesame oil
- soy sauce

Direction

- 1. If it's not cooked already, start the brown rice.
- 2. Wash and chop/dice all of the veggies for the stir-fry while you wait 20-25 minutes or so to let the rice cook.
- 3. Heat a wok on medium - medium high heat. After about a minute, coat it with sesame oil.
- 4. Add the diced vegetables and sesame seeds in whatever order you prefer. I was real hungry so I added them all at once and it came out fine. ;)
- 5. Stirring continuously, add maybe about a tablespoon of soy sauce.
- 6. Add a about a teaspoon or more each of ginger and curry powder.
- 7. When the veggies are cooked to your liking, add the rice, stirring to coat it with all of the oil/spices. Do a taste test and add more spice or soy sauce as necessary.

17. Day Old Fried Rice Recipe

Serving: 4 | Prep: | Cook: 10mins | Ready in:

Ingredients

- Day old cooked sticky rice
- 3-4 slices cooked pork bacon cut into 1 inch pieces
- 2 scrambled eggs cut into 2" strips or 1/2" chunks
- 2 TBSP soy sauce (eyeball it)
- Pam cooking spray
- Frying pan
- Spatula

Direction

- Spray Pam on your hot frying pan.
- Sauté rice while adding soy sauce gradually until rice turns light brown.
- Cook it enough to just heat it through.
- Remove from heat.
- Add precut pieces of bacon and eggs and fold into fried rice.
- And serve.

18. Easy Chinese Fried Rice Recipe

Serving: 0 | Prep: | Cook: 17mins | Ready in:

Ingredients

- 2 eggs, beaten
- oil (peanut/vegetable/sunflower)
- 8 ounces cooked chicken, chopped
- ¾ cup finely chopped onion
- 4 spring onions, finely chopped
- 2 tsps minced ginger and garlic
- ½ cup frozen mixed veggies
- 4 cups cold cooked rice(break up lumps and crumble with your fingers)
- 1 chicken stock cube dissolved in around 2 tbsp water
- 1 tbsp dark soy sauce
- 2 tsp light soy sauce
- 2 tsp sesame oil
- freshly ground black pepper

Direction

- Heat oil in a wok; add chopped onions and stir-fry until onions turn a nice brown color, about 8-10 minutes; remove from wok.
- Mix egg with 3 drops of light soy and 3 drops of sesame oil, set aside.

- Add oil to wok, add egg mixture; working quickly, when egg puffs, flip egg and cook other side briefly; remove from wok, and chop into small pieces.
- Heat 1 tbsp. oil in wok; add chicken to wok, along with onions, ginger, garlic, ground black pepper, the dissolved chicken stock and mixed veggies; stir-fry for 2 minutes.
- Add rice and spring onions, tossing to mix well; stir-fry for 3 minutes.
- Add 2 tbsp. of light & dark soy sauce and chopped egg to rice mixture and fold in; stir-fry for 1 minute more.
- Serve hot!

19. Easy Fried Rice Recipe

Serving: 4 | Prep: | Cook: 15mins | Ready in:

Ingredients

- 4 cups white rice, prepared
- 2 tablespoon sesame or vegetable oil
- 2 eggs, lightly beaten
- 1 onion, finely chopped
- 3 cloves garlic, finely chopped
- 1 cup frozen peas, thawed
- 4 tablespoons soy sauce (i like to use a lot, but you can add less)
- salt and pepper to taste

Direction

- Prepare rice as directed. Set aside to cool (if possible, refrigerate overnight).
- Heat a little oil in frying pan over medium heat. Add eggs, scramble until cooked, remove and set aside.
- Add the rest of the oil to the pan, heat. Add the garlic and onion, cook until soft, season with salt and pepper.
- Add the rice, break up any clumps and toss to coat with oil.
- Stir in soy sauce, peas, and cooked eggs. Cook until heated through and nicely fried.

20. Easy Indonesian Fried Rice Nasi Goreng Recipe

Serving: 0 | Prep: | Cook: 17mins | Ready in:

Ingredients

- 4 cups cold cooked rice(break up lumps and crumble with your fingers)
- 2 tbsp tamarind paste
- vegetable oil
- 8 shallots, chopped
- 3 cloves garlic, crushed
- ½ inch fresh ginger, grated
- 2 tsp curry powder
- ¼ tsp hot red pepper flakes
- ¼ tsp turmeric
- ½ small cabbage, thinly sliced
- 2 medium tomatoes, peeled, seeded, and diced
- 3 tbsp soy sauce
- 1 tbsp brown sugar
- To Garnish
- 3 tomatoes, coarsely chopped
- 1 ¼ red peppers, cored, seeded, and diced
- ½ cucumber, diced
- 1 stalk celery, diced
- Omelette cut into strips

Direction

- Stir in the tamarind paste with the rice and set aside.
- Heat some oil in a wok or skillet, add the shallots, and cook for 3-5 minutes, until softened.
- Add the garlic, ginger, curry powder, pepper flakes, and turmeric and cook gently, stirring, for 1 minute.
- Add the cabbage and cook for 3-5 minutes.
- Add the tomatoes and cook for 2-3 minutes.
- Remove from pan.
- Heat more oil in the wok, add the rice, and cook gently until lightly browned.

- Return the vegetables to the pan.
- Add the soy sauce and sugar and heat gently to warm through.
- Serve hot, garnished with tomatoes, red pepper, cucumber, celery, and omelet strips.

21. Egg Fried Rice Recipe

Serving: 2 | Prep: | Cook: 10mins | Ready in:

Ingredients

- 400g cooked white rice
- 1 tablespoon olive oil
- 5 spring onions, finely chopped
- 4 cloves of garlic, finely sliced
- 1 egg
- 50g peas (garden peas or petit pois)
- 2 teaspoons soy sauce

Direction

- Heat the oil in the wok.
- Fry the spring onions and garlic for 40 seconds.
- Add the rice and stir-fry for two minutes.
- Splash the soy sauce over the rice.
- Pour the egg on top off the rice and mix well.
- Serve and enjoy.

22. Egg Fried Rice With Chicken And Prawns Recipe

Serving: 4 | Prep: | Cook: 20mins | Ready in:

Ingredients

- 200g pure basmati rice, rinsed
- 2 tablespoons sweet chilli sauce
- 2 tablespoons light soy sauce
- 1 tablespoon toasted sesame oil
- 1 and a 1/2 tablespoons sesame seeds
- 1 tablespoon sunflower oil
- 1 free-range chicken breast, cut into 2cm cubes
- 130g raw peeled king prawns
- 50g mangetout, cut in half
- 1/2 red pepper, sliced
- 3 spring onions, sliced
- 1 large clove of garlic, peeled and crushed
- 20g knob of fresh ginger, peeled and grated
- 2 large free-range eggs, beaten
- 2 handfuls of roughly chopped coriander

Direction

- Bring a large saucepan of water to the boil, add the basmati rice, stir once, and bring back to the boil.
- When the rice comes to the boil, it will appear to be 'dancing in the water' and this is when the timer should be started and the rice boiled for eight minutes or until al dente.
- Place the rice in a sieve, cover with a sheet of kitchen towel and allow to stand for five minutes to absorb any excess water.
- Meanwhile, mix the sweet chilli sauce together with the soy sauce and the toasted sesame oil and set aside.
- Heat a wok over a high heat until nearly smoking. Add the sesame seeds and stir-fry for 30 seconds until browned, then remove.
- Add the oil and swirl around the wok to heat through. Stir-fry the chicken for one minute before adding the prawns and cooking for another 1 and a 1/2 minutes. Remove and place in another sieve for any excess oil to drain away.
- To the wok, add the mange tout and red pepper with two tablespoons of water, and stir-fry for 1 and a 1/2 minutes with a lid on if you have one.
- Add the basmati rice, spring onion, garlic and ginger and stir-fry for a further two minutes.
- Move the rice to the side of the wok and pour the egg onto the base of the wok. The egg should be in quite large pieces, so resist the temptation to mix it in too soon.
- Leave for 30 seconds to set a little before stirring through the rice with the chicken,

- prawns, and two-thirds of the coriander, the sauce and the sesame seeds.
- Toss to mix everything thoroughly and serve immediately. Sprinkle with the remaining coriander.

23. Elaines Chinese Fried Rice Recipe

Serving: 6 | Prep: | Cook: 30mins | Ready in:

Ingredients

- 2 cups brown rice
- 3 cups chicken stock
- 1 lemon
- 3 tbsp KIKKOMAN soy sauce (to me, this brand is the cadillac!)
- 4 tbsp canola oil
- 1 tbsp butter
- 2 medium sized carrots, finely cut
- 1 medium sized onion, finely chopped
- 1 large stalk celery, finely chopped
- 1/2 cup fresh or frozen peas
- 1/4 red pepper (sweet) finely chopped
- 2 cloves garlic, finely minced
- 4 tbsp fresh chives, finely chopped (or 3 tbsp dried)
- 1 tbsp Chinese five-spice mixture
- 1/2 tsp vanilla extract
- 1 tsp rice flour
- 1 egg
- salt and pepper to taste

Direction

- Prepare the rice by boiling in the chicken stock until el dente (still having some bite to it)
- Remove rice from pot RESERVING the liquid
- Transfer the rice to a deep frying pan or wok
- Before proceeding further, bring the stock to the boil, adding one whole lemon, cut in half to release its juices
- Continue boiling the stock on high heat, removing the lemon halves after 10 minutes.
- Boil the stock down to a reduction of 1/2 the original quantity.
- While the stock reduces:
- To the rice in the wok, add the oil, butter, Chinese five-spice, and soy sauce
- Mix well
- Heat should be medium to avoid scorching, and mixture should be stirred often
- Add the vanilla
- Crazy as this sounds, the vanilla serves to heighten the flavor of this dish
- Add the carrots, celery, onions, garlic, red pepper and peas, combining thoroughly and stirring frequently
- Now:
- Break one whole egg separately and whisk until well combined
- Add SLOWLY to the rice so it does not cook immediately in clumps like you see in egg foo young
- Add half the chives; reserve the other half for garnishing
- When the stock is reduced, add it to the mixture
- Add the rice flour, and stir well to help thicken the remaining reduction
- Add salt and pepper to taste, and serve.
- ENJOY!

24. Emelis Seafood Fried Rice Recipe

Serving: 5 | Prep: | Cook: 15mins | Ready in:

Ingredients

- 1 1/2 pounds of raw shrimp
- 1 1/2 pounds of raw lobster
- 1 pound of crab
- 1/2 pound of scallon
- 4 cups of cooked rice
- 1 egg

- 1 scallion
- 1 pound of pork barbecue
- salt and pepper for tasting
- 1 clove of garlic
- vegetable oil

Direction

- Heat 2 tbs of oil in wok. Medium heat. Once heated, add egg; stirring until softly scrambled. Set aside
- Add all the seafood and garlic, stirring for 2 minutes. Set aside seafood, leaving garlic in wok
- Stir in rice and pork barbecue ad mix with the tasty brown bits left from the seafood.
- Once rice is completely fried, mix everything and set on plate.
- Add salt, pepper, and sprinkle shredded scallion
- Serve with soy sauce

25. FRIED RICE AND PASTA Recipe

Serving: 712 | Prep: | Cook: 20mins | Ready in:

Ingredients

- vegetable cooking spray
- 1/4 c. thinly sliced celery
- 1/4 c. thinly sliced green onions
- 1 tbsp. reduced calorie margarine
- 1/2 c. long grain rice, uncooked
- 2 oz. vermicelli, uncooked & broken into 1/2" pieces
- 2 c. hot water
- 1 tbsp. chopped fresh parsley
- 1/2 tsp. chicken-flavored bouillon granules
- 1/4 tsp. salt
- 1/4 tsp. garlic powder

Direction

- Coat a large nonstick skillet with cooking spray; place over medium-high heat until hot. Add celery and onions; sauté until tender. Transfer to a serving bowl and set aside. Coat skillet with cooking spray; add margarine and place over medium heat until margarine melts.
- Stir in rice and vermicelli; cook over medium heat until vermicelli is lightly browned, stirring frequently. Add water, sautéed celery and onions and remaining ingredients to rice mixture. Cover, reduce heat and simmer 15-20 minutes or until rice is tender and liquid is absorbed. Stir before serving.
- Yield 7 servings. (1/2 cup serving)
- Weight Watcher Points - 2 Points

26. Fancy Pineapple Thai Fried Rice Recipe

Serving: 46 | Prep: | Cook: 10mins | Ready in:

Ingredients

- 1 tablespoon minced garlic
- 1/3 cup peanut oil
- 1 lb. black tiger shrimp
- (peeled and deveined)
- 1/3 cup diced carrot
- 1/3 cup diced onion
- 1 egg (beaten)
- 4 cups cooked jasmine rice
- 1 tablespoon butter
- 1 teaspoon sea salt
- 1 teaspoon sugar
- 1 teaspoon white pepper
- 1/3 cup sweet peas
- 1/3 cup raisin
- 4 tablespoons soy sauce
- 1 fresh pineapple (cut in half,
- remove fruit, cut into chunks)
- 1/3 cup roasted cashews

Direction

- In a wok at medium-high heat, add the garlic and oil and stir until golden brown. Add the shrimp and cook for 3 more minutes, stirring occasionally. Follow with carrot and onion, stirring for 2 minutes
- Add the beaten egg and stir constantly for 30 seconds. Add rice, butter, salt, sugar, white pepper, sweet pea, raisin, soy sauce and fresh pineapple and stir until the ingredients are thoroughly mixed, approximately 3 minutes. Remove from heat, place in hollowed-out pineapple halves and top with cashews before serving.

27. Fast Fried Rice Recipe

Serving: 6 | Prep: | Cook: 10mins | Ready in:

Ingredients

- 3 Cups cooked white rice
- 5 slices bacon, cut into 1/2 in pieces (for flavor and the oil)
- You can omit the bacon, just add 3 Tbs of sesame or veg oil for first step, with the onion.
- 3/4 Cup Coarsley chopped onion
- 4 Tbs light soy sauce
- 1 cup bean sprouts
- 1 cup frozen peas
- 1/4 Cup minced peanuts
- 1/2 Cup Diced fresh carrots
- 2 eggs, beaten slightly
- 3 Tbs Chopped green onion, tops only
- Optional chicken, sausage, Veggies or beef

Direction

- Partially cook bacon in large wok or skillet. Add onion, cook until tender but not brown.
- Stir in cooked rice and soy sauce, cook until heated through, stirring occasionally. Add Peas, carrots, sprouts and peanuts.
- Push rice to side. Pour egg into middle of the pan. Stir quick to scramble, until done. Stir egg into rice and blend.
- Add green onion and any additional cooked ingredients (chicken, sausage, beef, shrimp or vegetables)
- Ready!

28. Fast Veggie Stir Fry Recipe

Serving: 1 | Prep: | Cook: 10mins | Ready in:

Ingredients

- 1 cup cooked white rice
- 1 Tbs. vegetable oil
- 1/4 cup chopped onions
- 2 Tbs. soy sauce
- 1/4 cup finely diced carrots
- 1/4 cup diced green peppers

Direction

- 1. Add vegetable oil and onions into a wok or skillet. Cook until the onions are tender not brown.
- 2. Stir in cooked rice and soy sauce. Cook until heated through, stirring occasionally.
- 3. Add carrots and green peppers and a sprinkle of salt and pepper. Give it a stir.
- 4. Then enjoy!

29. Favorite Fried Rice Recipe

Serving: 4 | Prep: | Cook: 15mins | Ready in:

Ingredients

- 4 Cups cooked rice, room temperature
- 1/2 Cup Chopped green onion
- 1/2 Cup Diced Cooked carrots
- 1/2 Teaspoon Peeled minced ginger
- 2 Pressed Medium garlic cloves
- 1/4 Cup Diced green bell pepper
- 1/4 Cup Diced red bell pepper
- 1 egg, beaten

- 3 Tablespoons Black sesame oil
- soy sauce to taste
- white pepper
- 1 Cup Diced cooked chicken or pork cut in 1/2" pieces *optional

Direction

- Heat 2 tablespoons of the black sesame oil in a wok or large skillet over medium to medium high heat.
- Add green onions, ginger, red & green peppers and garlic and stir fry until fragrant (about 3 minutes).
- Add optional meat and cook for a couple minutes until heated.
- Add carrots and fold in rice, and stir fry for about 10 minutes, adding the extra tablespoon of sesame oil to taste until rice takes on a light tan coloring from the oil.
- Add soy sauce to taste (no more than 1.5 Tablespoons unless you like it really salty) and mix well.
- Push mixture to the side of the wok or pan and scramble the egg in the open area of the pan.
- Fold egg into rice mixture, season with white pepper to taste, and serve.

30. Fried Forbidden Rice Recipe

Serving: 6 | Prep: | Cook: 85mins | Ready in:

Ingredients

- 1 head of garlic (about 12 cloves) cloves peeled
- 2 tbs vegetable oil, plus more for drizzling
- 2 cups black rice (black or forbidden rice is available at Asian specialty stores or on Amazon.com)
- 2 cups water
- 1/4 lb lean bacon, coarsely chopped
- 1 medium onion, cut into 1/2-inch dice
- 1/4 cup soy sauce or tamari
- salt and freshly ground white pepper
- 4 scallions, coarsely chopped

Direction

- Preheat the oven to 350 degrees. Put the garlic cloves on a double sheet of foil and drizzle with vegetable oil. Seal the foil around the garlic and bake for about 1 hour, until the garlic is soft and caramelized. Let cool, then refrigerate overnight.
- Meanwhile, in a saucepan, cover the black rice with water and bring to a boil.
- Cover and cook over low heat for about 20 minutes, until the water is absorbed and the rice is tender. Remove from the heat and let stand, covered for about 10 minutes. Spread the rice on a large rimmed baking sheet and let cool to room temperature. Cover and refrigerate overnight.
- In a large, deep skillet, cook the bacon over moderate heat until crisp, about 6 minutes. Using a slotted spoon, transfer bacon to a plate.
- Pour off all of the fat in the skillet and add 2 tbs of oil. Add the onion and cook over moderate heat, stirring occasionally, until softened, about 6 minutes. Stir in the bacon, black rice and roasted garlic and stir-fry over moderately high heat until warmed through, about 3 minutes. Stir in the soy sauce and season with salt and white pepper. Transfer to bowls, garnish with the scallions and serve right away.

31. Fried Rice Noodle Recipe

Serving: 2 | Prep: | Cook: 5mins | Ready in:

Ingredients

- 500 grams kwetiao, rice noodle
- 100 grams of pork, thinly sliced
- 1/2 teaspoon sugar
- 2 tbs of minced garlic
- 1 chilli
- 1 egg
- 2 tbs soy sauce

- 2 tbs oyster sauce
- 1 tbs fish sauce (optional)
- salt and pepper to taste

Direction

- In a wok heat a little oil
- Add pork, stir fry until golden brown
- Add garlic, chilli, until fragrant put sugar to caramelized
- Then you can add the egg, scramble until egg is done
- Add soy sauce keep stirring until you smell a smoky flavor
- Stir in your noodles add the rest of the ingredients
- Keep stirring until all noodles are coated by soy sauce
- Add bean sprout, mix well, and serve

32. Fried Rice Recipe

Serving: 2 | Prep: | Cook: 20mins | Ready in:

Ingredients

- Fresh cooked rice (I don't use overnight rice because the kids are eating)
- Long beans, diced
- baby corn, diced
- carrot, diced
- Fake crabmeat (similar to crab stick; it's made from fish paste)
- egg
- salt to taste

Direction

- Stir fried long beans, baby corn, carrot and fake crabmeat till cooked.
- Set aside.
- Scramble an egg till cooked.
- Add in cooked rice and the earlier cooked ingredients.
- Add salt to taste.

- Continue to stir fried till mixed well.
- Dish and serve.

33. Fried Rice With Lobster Recipe

Serving: 4 | Prep: | Cook: 5mins | Ready in:

Ingredients

- 1 small lobster
- 1 egg
- 2 cups cooked rice
- 2 fresh or canned mushrooms diced
- 1 teaspoon soy sauce
- 1 diced peeled water chestnut

Direction

- Boil lobster for 10 minutes then remove and dice meat.
- Scramble egg in a hot greased skillet until slightly brown.
- Mix lobster, egg and remaining ingredient then fry in oil for 5 minutes.

34. Fried Rice With Tofu Recipe

Serving: 2 | Prep: | Cook: 30mins | Ready in:

Ingredients

- 2 cups cooked rice
- 1 lrg. onion, sliced
- 1 green pepper, sliced
- 2 ribs celery, sliced
- 1/2 lb. tofu, diced
- 2 tbsp soy sauce
- 2 green onions, cut into 1/2 inch slices

Direction

- In skillet or wok heat some oil

- Add tofu cubes and soy sauce and stir-fry for 1 minute
- REMOVE tofu and to the same skillet add 2 tbsp. oil, onion, green pepper, and celery. Stir-fry this for 3-4 minutes.
- Slowly add the cooked rice
- Add soy sauce and tofu cubes.
- Stir-fry until hot. Serve topped with green onions.

35. Fried Rice With Bacon Recipe

Serving: 6 | Prep: | Cook: 25mins | Ready in:

Ingredients

- Fried Rice with bacon
- Ingredients
- 2 medium leeks (white portion only), chopped
- 1 medium onion, chopped
- 2 tablespoons olive oil
- 4-1/2 cups cooked rice
- 1/2 teaspoon salt
- 1 egg, lightly beaten (an option)
- 5 bacon strips, cooked and crumbled
- Pepper to taste

Direction

- (The egg would be an option)
- Directions
- 1. In a large skillet, sauté leeks and onion in oil until tender, about 10 minutes. Add the rice and salt; cook until lightly browned, stirring frequently. Quickly stir in the egg until blended; cook and stir until egg is completely cooked. Sprinkle with the bacon and pepper. Yield: 6 servings.
- TOTAL TIME: Prep/Total Time: 25 min.
- MAKES: 6 servings

36. Garlic Fried Rice Recipe

Serving: 4 | Prep: | Cook: 10mins | Ready in:

Ingredients

- 4 cups cooked rice - preferably cold or left over
- 2 tbsp cloves garlic - minced
- 2 tbsp vegetable oil
- 1 cup frozen mixed vegetables (optional)
- 1 1/2 kosher salt
- black pepper to taste

Direction

- Heat oil in a wok or large skillet over medium heat
- Add garlic. Cook until golden brown but not burn
- Add frozen vegetables if using. Cook for 3 minutes or until vegetables are no longer frozen
- Add rice, salt and black pepper and mix well. Cook for about 5 minutes mixing occasionally to prevent burning.
- Serve hot.

37. Ginger Fried Rice Recipe

Serving: 4 | Prep: | Cook: 10mins | Ready in:

Ingredients

- 1/2 cup peanut oil
- 2 tablespoons minced garlic
- 2 tablespoons minced ginger
- salt
- 2 cups thinly sliced leeks, white and light green parts only, rinsed and dried
- 4 cups day-old cooked rice; Vongerichten recommends jasmine but this is the perfect way to use up any leftover rice you have, especially from Chinese delivery
- 4 large eggs

- 2 teaspoons sesame oil (for some heat but the same awesome
- flavor, use hot sesame oil)
- 4 teaspoons soy sauce

Direction

- In a large skillet, heat 1/4 cup oil over medium heat.
- Add garlic and ginger and cook, stirring occasionally, until crisp and brown.
- With a slotted spoon, transfer to paper towels and salt lightly.
- Reduce heat under skillet to medium-low and add 2 tablespoons oil and leeks.
- Cook about 10 minutes, stirring occasionally, until very tender but not browned.
- Season lightly with salt.
- Raise heat to medium and add rice.
- Cook, stirring well, until heated through. Season to taste with salt.
- In a non-stick skillet (it just makes it easier) fry eggs in remaining oil, sunny-side-up, until edges are set but yolk is still runny.
- Divide rice among four dishes.
- Top each with an egg and drizzle with 1/2 teaspoon sesame oil and 1 teaspoon soy sauce.
- Sprinkle crisped garlic and ginger over everything and serve.

38. Ginger Fried Rice With Shitake Mushrooms Recipe

Serving: 6 | Prep: | Cook: 25mins | Ready in:

Ingredients

- 2 tablespoons plus 1 teaspoon vegetable oil
- 1 large egg, beaten with 1 tablespoon water
- 1 1/2 tablespoons minced peeled fresh ginger
- 3 scallions, white and green parts chopped separately
- 3/4 teaspoon kosher salt
- 1/2 lb fresh shiitake mushrooms, stems discarded and caps thinly sliced
- 3 cups cold cooked white rice
- 1/2 teaspoon Asian sesame oil

Direction

- Heat a wok or a 12-inch non-stick skillet over moderate heat until hot, then add 1/2 teaspoon vegetable oil and swirl around wok. Add half of egg mixture and swirl wok to coat bottom with a thin layer about 5 inches in diameter. When egg crêpe is set, about 45 seconds, transfer with a wide metal spatula to a plate to cool. Make another egg crêpe with another 1/2 teaspoon vegetable oil and remaining egg mixture in same manner. Stack crêpes, roll into a cylinder, and cut crosswise into 1/4-inch-wide strips, then unroll.
- Heat remaining 2 tablespoons vegetable oil in wok over high heat until it begins to smoke. Add ginger, white part of scallions, and salt and stir-fry until fragrant, about 30 seconds. Add shiitakes and stir-fry until tender, 3 to 5 minutes. Crumble rice into wok and stir-fry until lightly browned, 10 to 15 minutes. Remove from heat and add scallion greens, egg strips, and sesame oil, tossing to combine.

39. Golden Fried Rice Recipe

Serving: 2 | Prep: | Cook: 10mins | Ready in:

Ingredients

- 2 cups of cooked rice
- 4 tablespoon of thinly sliced garlic
- 2 tablespoon of olive oil
- 1 egg
- 1/8 teaspoon of salt

Direction

- Heat the oil, add in the garlic.
- Fry till golden, add in the rice and fry for 2 mins.
- Leave a hole in the middle and beat the egg to it.

- Cover the egg with rice. Stir after 30 seconds and mix well till the egg coat almost all the rice.
- Constantly stir till the rice is dry and can pop on the wok.
- Ready to serve.

40. Hibachi Style Fried Rice Recipe

Serving: 6 | Prep: | Cook: 15mins | Ready in:

Ingredients

- 4 Cups white rice (cooked)
- 1 Whole white onion (chopped)
- 2 eggs (beaten)
- 1 Tablespoon garlic (minced)
- 2 green onion (aka spring onions, chopped)
- 4 Tablespoons dark soy sauce
- 2 Tablespoons sesame oil
- 2 Tablespoons mirin (sweet rice wine)
- 3 Tablespoons cooking oil
- Alternatives include:
- 2 Tablespoons rice wine (for the mirin)
- 4 oz Protein (your choice)

Direction

- Prepare all your ingredients in advance, as stir-fry cooking is very fast and you won't have time to measure once the cooking starts!
- Pour your cooking oil (not the sesame oil) into your Wok and heat it up (medium-high for most ranges).
- Add chopped onion and garlic (and any optional protein), stir constantly for 2 minutes. Onion should be softened and becoming clear, while the garlic is nicely browning.
- Add beaten egg and stir until the egg becomes solid. It should still be slightly moist.
- Add rice and stir well immediately to ensure it all receives some oil coating.
- Add soy, mirin, sesame, and green onion. Cooking until hot.
- Serve immediately.

41. How To Make Egg Fried Rice Recipe

Serving: 3 | Prep: | Cook: 45mins | Ready in:

Ingredients

- • 2 cup rice Soaked and Drained
- • 2 eggs, Lightly Beaten
- • 2 onion, Sliced
- • 1-2 carrot, Peeled and Chopped
- • 1 Medium Sized capsicum, Chopped
- • ¼ cup cabbage, Chopped
- • ½ cup peas, Finely Chopped
- • 2-3 green chilies, Chopped
- • 1 tsp ginger, Chopped
- • 1 tsp garlic, Chopped
- • ¼ tsp white pepper powder
- • 1 Bunch green onion, Chopped
- • 1-2 tbsp soya sauce
- • 1 tbsp lime juice
- • oil for fry
- • salt to taste

Direction

- Step 1: Boil rice in a pan add salt and cook till the rice is tender. Turn off the heat, drain well and let them cool
- Step 2: Heat oil in a pan, add onion, green chilies, garlic and ginger. Stir it for few minutes till the onion become soften

42. INDONESIAN FRIED RICE NASI GORENG Recipe

Serving: 4 | Prep: | Cook: 40mins | Ready in:

Ingredients

- To rinse the rice, you can either place it in a fine-mesh strainer and rinse under cool water or place it in a medium bowl and repeatedly fill the bowl with water while swishing the rice around, then carefully drain off the water. In either case, you must rinse until the water runs clear. Adjust the spiciness of this dish by including the minced ribs and seeds from the chiles.
- Sweet soy sauce Kecap manis, a dark brown, syrupy-thick Indonesian sauce, is often called sweet soy sauce. It is sweetened with palm sugar and sometimes seasoned with various other ingredients, such as garlic and star anise. In Indonesia it's used in marinades, as a flavoring in dishes and as a condiment. Kecap manis can be found in Asian markets and stored indefinitely in a cool, dry place.
- 3 1/3 cups water
- 2 1/2 cups jasmine, basmati, or other long-grain white rice , rinsed (see note)
- 6 fresh Thai, serrano, or jalapeño chiles , seeds and ribs removed, chiles minced (see note)
- 4 large shallots , peeled and quartered
- 4 medium garlic cloves , peeled
- 6 tablespoons vegetable oil
- 1/4 cup sweet soy sauce (see below), plus extra for serving
- salt
- 1 medium cucumber , peeled, halved lengthwise, and sliced 1/2 inch thick
- 2 large plum tomatoes , cored and sliced into 1/2-inch-thick rounds
- 4 large eggs , cracked into 2 small bowls (2 eggs per bowl)
- ground black pepper
- 4 medium scallions , sliced thin
- 1 recipe Fried shallots (see related recipe) (optional)

Direction

- 1. Bring the water and rice to a boil in a large Dutch oven over high heat. Reduce the heat to low, cover, and cook until all the water has been absorbed, about 15 minutes. Remove the pot from the heat and let it sit, covered, until the rice is tender, about 15 minutes. Spread the cooked rice out over a baking sheet and let cool to room temperature, about 30 minutes. (The rice can be transferred to an airtight container and refrigerated for up to 24 hours.)
- 2. Meanwhile, pulse the chiles, shallots, and garlic together in a food processor to a coarse paste, about 15 pulses, stopping to scrape down the sides of the bowl as needed; set aside.
- 3. Break up any large clumps of cooled rice with your fingers. Heat 1/4 cup of the oil in a 12-inch nonstick skillet over medium heat until just shimmering. Add the processed chile mixture and cook until the shallots become translucent and the moisture evaporates, 3 to 5 minutes. Increase the heat to medium-high and add the rice, sweet soy sauce, and 1 1/2 teaspoons salt. Cook, stirring constantly to break up any rice clumps, until the rice is heated through and evenly coated, about 5 minutes.
- 4. Portion the rice onto individual plates and garnish with the cucumber and tomatoes. Wipe the skillet clean with a wad of paper towels, add the remaining 2 tablespoons oil to the skillet, and return to medium-high heat until shimmering. Following the illustration below, quickly add the eggs to the skillet. Season the eggs with salt and pepper, cover, and cook until the whites are set but the yolks are still runny, 2 to 3 minutes.
- 5. Uncover the eggs and remove from the heat. Carefully slide one egg over each plate of rice. Sprinkle with the scallions and fried shallots (if using) and serve.

43. Improvised Thai Stir Fried Rice Recipe

Serving: 2 | Prep: | Cook: 8mins | Ready in:

Ingredients

- 1/2 cup cooked brown basmati rice - 3

- 1 cup cooked white jasmine rice - 3
- 1 clove garlic, minced - 1
- 1 egg, lightly beaten - 2
- 1 small carrot, shredded -3
- 3 tbsp chopped fresh cilantro -3
- 1/2 section of ginger - minced - 3
- 2 tbsp olive oil - 0
- 2 tbsp soy sauce -3
- salt & pepper to taste

Direction

- Heat oil until very hot in a wok or pan.
- Sauté garlic (1) 1+ minutes or until just turning brown.
- Add egg (2). Allow egg to cook for 30 seconds then stir to break up until fully cooked (about 1 minute).
- Add remaining ingredients (3): rice, carrot, cilantro, ginger and soy sauce. Cook 2 to 3 minutes.
- Remove from heat, salt and pepper to taste and serve.

44. Island Fried Rice Recipe

Serving: 4 | Prep: | Cook: 7mins | Ready in:

Ingredients

- 1 to 2 cups leftover rice
- 1 mango, skinned/seeded cut into small cubes
- 1 tomato, seeded, and diced
- 1/2 onion (preferably red, but any kind works)
- 1 green/yellow bell pepper, seeded/deribbed and diced
- 1/2 jalapeno, seeded/deribbed, and minced
- oil for frying

Direction

- Preheat a wok with a little oil over medium-high heat.
- Toss in jalapeno and bell pepper, sauté for one minute.
- Toss in red onion, sauté for one more minute.
- Throw in rice and stir to heat thoroughly.
- When rice becomes aromatic, add mango and tomato, stir to combine. Serve.

45. JDs Sardine Fried Rice Recipe

Serving: 2 | Prep: | Cook: 15mins | Ready in:

Ingredients

- approx. 1 tbsp. ghee or olive oil
- 2 cups cooked rice (medium-grain brown rice is good; we also use basmati)
- 2 cans of sardines in water or oil (approximately 4.25 oz each)
- approx. 1 tsp. soy sauce
- one squirt nam pla or similar fish sauce
- 2-4 tbsp. furikake, goma shio, or similar
- 2-4 large pinches of shredded nori
- 1/4 cup shredded pickled vegetables (standard Japanese or Thai pickled vegetables: daikon, carrot, et cetera — optional)

Direction

- Drain the sardines & break them apart with a fork. (If they're in oil, you may be able to use that for cooking — or, feed the drained liquid to your cat.)
- Place your wok or favorite frying/sauté pan on medium heat
- Add ghee or olive oil, wait for it to heat up
- Add rice, sardines, soy sauce, and nam pla
- Toss them together (still on medium heat) for 3-5 minutes, until fully heated
- Add vegetables (optional) and furikake; mix well
- Add shredded nori one pinch at a time, still mixing (otherwise it tends to clump up)
- Mix it all on the stove for another couple of minutes
- Serve & enjoy immediately

46. Laurie's Fried Rice Recipe

Serving: 4 | Prep: | Cook: 1hours | Ready in:

Ingredients

- 3 cups cooked white rice
- 3 tbs sesame oil
- 1 cup frozen peas and carrots (thawed)
- 1 small onion, chopped
- 1tsp minced garlic
- 2 eggs, slightly beaten
- 1/4 cup soy sauce

Direction

- Make rice per package directions. Let it come to room temp or for best results chill overnight, then bring to room temp.
- On medium high heat, heat the oil in a large skillet or wok.
- Add the peas, carrots, onion and garlic. Stir fry until tender.
- Lower the heat to medium low and push the mixture off to one side, then pour the eggs on the other side of skillet and stir fry until scrambled.
- Add the rice and soy sauce and blend all together well.
- Stir fry until thoroughly heated.

47. Leftover Ham Fried Rice Recipe

Serving: 8 | Prep: | Cook: 30mins | Ready in:

Ingredients

- 4 cups of Minute Rice, cooked (2 cup uncooked)(can also be cold leftover rice)
- 2 eggs, hard cooked scrambled in small pieces
- 1/2 med. onion, sauteed
- 1/2 jar sliced mushrooms
- 4 oz leftover ham, dices or in strips
- 1/4 soy sauce
- 1/2 water
- oil

Direction

- Pour 2 T. oil into large sauté pan or wok. Heat on medium high till ready. Add rice. Cook till heated through. Add onion, ham and mushrooms. Cook 2 minutes more. Stir in eggs. Mix soy sauce and water together. Gradually pour into rice mixture until it reaches a salt y soy flavor you like. Cook another 2 minutes or so, stirring continuously. Serve piping hot!!!

48. Mai Pen Rai Shrimp And Chicken Thai Fried Rice Recipe

Serving: 4 | Prep: | Cook: 15mins | Ready in:

Ingredients

- 12.5 oz. Can of chicken breast chunks
- 6 oz. Can shrimp (broken or the really tiny ones or larger ones)
- 2 T. oil
- ½ t. Minced garlic
- ¼ Cup Minced onion (or onion powder)
- 2 eggs (beaten)
- 2 Cups cooked rice
- 3 T. green peas (I use canned peas)
- 2 T. Chopped green onion
- 1 ½ T. fish sauce
- ½ T. oyster sauce
- ½ t. sugar
- 1 lime

Direction

- Heat oil then stir fry garlic & onion until fragrant.
- Add chicken and shrimp and stir-fry until mixed well.

- Add eggs and stir-fry until slightly solid.
- Add rice, then peas and green onions, then fish sauce, oyster sauce, and sugar.
- Stir well to mix.
- Squeeze on lime juice. Serve.

49. Making Fabulous Fried Rice Recipe

Serving: 0 | Prep: | Cook: 30mins | Ready in:

Ingredients

- • 4 cups cooked long or medium grain rice, leftover from the day before or refrigerated for at least 2 hours.
- • 1 Tbs. canola or other neutral oil.
- • 2 cloves garlic, minced.
- • 1/2 medium red or yellow onion, coarsely chopped (about 1/2 cup).
- • 1 cup carrots chopped into small pieces (about 2 medium).
- • 3 eggs.
- • 1 cup chopped leftover meat or tofu.
- • 1/2 cup frozen peas, defrosted.
- • 2 Tbs. oyster sauce (or sweet soy sauce).
- • 2 Tbs. soy sauce (or fish sauce).
- • Salt.
- • White pepper powder.

Direction

- 1. Break up large clumps of rice and separate the grains with wet fingers.
- 2. Preheat a 14-inch (35cm) wok or 12-inch (30cm) skillet over high heat for about 1 minute.
- 3. Swirl in the oil and heat until it becomes runny and starts to shimmer.
- 4. Reduce heat to medium and add garlic and onion and stir until fragrant, about 15 to 30 seconds. Add the carrots and cook until tender, about 2 to 3 minutes.
- 5. Move all the ingredients to one side of the wok. Break the eggs into the wok, and stir to scramble until they are almost cooked through but still a little soggy, about 1½ to 2 minutes.
- 6. Add the meat and the peas, followed by the rice, stirring and tossing between each addition. Use your spatula to break up any clumps.
- 7. Add the sauces, and salt and white pepper to taste. Stir everything swiftly around the wok until the rice is well-coated and -colored (little bits of white here and there is OK) and heated through, about 3 to 4 minutes. Add more oil if the rice begins to stick to the wok; reduce the heat if it starts to scorch. Taste and adjust seasonings if necessary.
- 8. Divide the rice among dinner plates. Serve immediately.

50. Mango Pork Fried Rice Recipe

Serving: 2 | Prep: | Cook: 5mins | Ready in:

Ingredients

- 3/4 cup diced cooked pork
- 1/2 teaspoon cornstarch
- 1 mango, peeled and diced (1 pound)
- 1 can (8 ounces) sliced water chestnuts, drained
- 1 cup sliced fresh mushrooms (3 ounces)
- 1 tablespoon finely chopped gingerroot
- 1 garlic clove, finely chopped
- 3 cups cold cooked rice
- 2 teaspoons reduced-sodium soy sauce
- 1 cup frozen green peas, thawed
- 2 medium green onions, sliced (2 tablespoons)
- 1/8 teaspoon pepper

Direction

- 1. Mix pork and cornstarch. Spray nonstick wok or 12-inch skillet with cooking spray; heat over medium-high heat until cooking spray starts to bubble. Add pork, mango, water chestnuts, mushrooms, gingerroot and garlic;

stir-fry 1 minute. Remove pork mixture from wok.
- 2. Spray wok or skillet with cooking spray; heat until cooking spray starts to bubble. Add rice; stir-fry about 1 minute or until rice is hot. Stir in soy sauce. Add pork mixture, peas, onions and pepper; stir-fry 1 minute. Serve.

breaking up chicken and roasted peppers as mixture cooks.
- Add cooked egg and rice; cook and stir 1 minute. Stir in taco sauce; cook 2 minutes or until thoroughly heated, stirring occasionally. Stir in green onions. Spoon mixture onto serving platter. Garnish with cilantro.

51. Mexican Fried Rice Recipe

Serving: 4 | Prep: | Cook: 20mins | Ready in:

Ingredients

- 1 cup uncooked jasmine rice
- 1 1/2 cups water
- 1 egg
- 1 tablespoon garlic-flavor olive oil or olive oil
- 1 pound fresh chicken tenders
- 1/2 cup chopped onion
- 2 cloves garlic, minced
- 1 (15 ounce) can black beans, drained
- 1 (11 ounce) can whole kernel corn, with Red and green peppers
- 1 (7 ounce) jar sliced roasted red bell peppers, drained
- 1 (8 ounce) jar taco sauce
- 1/4 cup chopped green onions
- 1/4 cup chopped fresh cilantro

Direction

- Cook rice in water as directed on package.
- Meanwhile, spray 12-inch skillet with non-stick cooking spray. Heat over medium heat until hot. Beat egg in small bowl. Add egg to skillet; cook 1 minute or until firm but still moist, stirring frequently. Remove from pan; cover to keep warm.
- Heat oil in same skillet over medium heat until hot. Add chicken, onion and garlic; cook and stir 4 to 6 minutes or until chicken is no longer pink in centre. Add beans, corn and roasted peppers; mix well. Cook 1 minute or until thoroughly heated, stirring constantly and

52. Millies Fried Rice Recipe

Serving: 4 | Prep: | Cook: 20mins | Ready in:

Ingredients

- 3 Cups cooked long grain rice, (not instant)
- 4 Tbs vegetable oil
- 1 medium onion, chopped
- 3 cloves garlic, minced
- 2 Tbs soy sauce
- 1 tsp salt
- 1/2 to 1 tsp black pepper, to taste
- 1 tsp sugar
- 1/2 Cup frozen vegetables, peas, corn, carrot, whatever you have on hand.

Direction

- Heat oil in pan. Medium high.
- Stir fry onions and garlic till onions are clear, be sure to not overcook garlic, when it starts to smell nutty, then you are close to over cooking.
- Add soy sauce, salt, pepper, and sugar.
- Slowly add rice a little at a time, stirring constantly till rice is uniform in color.
- Add in frozen veggies. Still stirring.
- Stir fry till veggies are heated through.
- Enjoy!!

53. Minced Beef Fried Rice Recipe

Serving: 4 | Prep: | Cook: 10mins | Ready in:

Ingredients

- 2 Tbs. soy sauce
- 1/2 tsp. sugar
- 1 Tbs. vegetable oil
- 3 eggs, well beaten
- 1/2 lb. minced lean beef
- 1/4 cups shredded iceberg lettuce
- 1/4 cups of frozen peas
- 1 celery, finely chopped
- 1 green onion, chopped
- 1 tsp. fresh ginger, minced
- 1 clove garlic, minced
- 2.5 cups cooked rice, cold

Direction

- Combine soy sauce, sugar and salt and pepper to taste in a small bowl and set aside.
- Heat oil in a wok or nonstick skillet over medium high heat.
- Cook eggs about 45 seconds, stirring constantly, until eggs are just set. Transfer eggs to a bowl.
- Add beef and sauté for a few minutes
- Add lettuce, peas, celery and onion to same skillet over medium heat. Sauté about 3 minutes, stirring often to break up meat, until browned.
- Stir in ginger and garlic and cook 1 minute.
- Remove excess fat and liquid that forms once beef is cooked.
- Increase heat to high and add rice. Stir-fry about 1 minute, until heated through.
- Stir in soy sauce mixture and eggs and stir-fry 30 seconds longer.

54. Moms Fried Rice Recipe

Serving: 4 | Prep: | Cook: 25mins | Ready in:

Ingredients

- 1 tsp canola oil
- 1 egg, beaten
- 8 strips bacon, chopped
- 1 c chopped fresh mushrooms
- 8 green onions, thinly sliced
- 3 c leftover rice
- 1 c bean sprouts
- 1 c frozen peas, thawed
- 1/4 c reduced-sodium soy sauce

Direction

- In large skillet, heat oil over med-high heat. Pour egg in pan. As egg sets, lift edges 'letting uncooked portion flow underneath. When egg is completely cooked, remove to plate; set aside.
- In same skillet, cook bacon over med. heat until crisp. Using a slotted spoon, remove to paper towels; drain, reserving 2 Tbs. drippings. Sauté mushrooms and onions in drippings.
- Stir in the rice, bean sprouts, peas, soy sauce and bacon. Chop egg into small pieces; stir into pan and heat through.

55. Multi Flavored Thai Fried Rice Recipe

Serving: 4 | Prep: | Cook: 10mins | Ready in:

Ingredients

- 3 cups jasmine rice
- 7 oz. pork loin (sliced thin & lengths approx. 2 inches long)
- 6 large shrimp (uncooked)
- 3 large eggs
- 2 slices boiled ham (diced)
- 1/3 cup sweet red pepper (diced)
- 1/4 cup sweet green pepper (diced)
- 1/2 cup mixed vegetables
- 1/3 cup black raisins
- 1 cup pineapple chunks
- 2 tbsp. soy sauce
- 3 tbsp. brown sugar
- 1 tbsp. garlic (chopped)

- 1 tbsp. paprika
- 3 tbsp. olive oil

Direction

- Using a rice cooker, or other method, cook the rice prior to starting this recipe.
- Wash the pork and slice it thin into 2 inch long strips.
- Heat the olive oil in a pan, add the garlic and fry until golden brown.
- Then, add the pork and stir for several minutes until well done.
- Add the shrimp to the pan and continue to stir until the shrimp turns pink, then add the ham and stir the pork, shrimp and ham together for a few minutes.
- Add the mixed vegetables, pineapple, raisins, sweet red pepper, green pepper, paprika and rice to the pan, then stir and mix everything thoroughly for a few minutes.
- Add the soy sauce and sugar to the pan and continue to stir frequently until well done (approx. 5 minutes), then remove from the heat.
- .
- Place a leaf of romaine lettuce and some sliced cucumber on each plate and then add the contents of the pan onto each plate.
- Garnish with coriander.
- Note: one can sub chicken for the pork or other fish or seafood for the shrimp
- Tip: If desired, fry one egg for each serving and place on each plate and season the egg with black pepper.

56. Mushroom Fried Rice Recipe

Serving: 2 | Prep: | Cook: 10mins | Ready in:

Ingredients

- 1 shallot chopped
- 3 garlic chopped
- 4 pieces of dried chinese mushroom (soaked and sliced)
- 1 cup of cold rice
- 1 egg
- 1 pinch of salt
- 1 pinch of pepper
- 1 teaspoon of oil

Direction

- Sauté shallot for 1/2min. Add in garlic and sauté till fragrant.
- Stir in mushroom and fry for a while before adding in the rice.
- Once the rice heat up add in the egg salt and pepper. Stir evenly.
- Dish and serve.

57. Mushrooms And Anchovies Fried Rice Recipe

Serving: 1 | Prep: | Cook: 5mins | Ready in:

Ingredients

- 1 bowl of rice
- 1 bowl of chopped mushrooms
- 1 egg
- 1 spring onion, finely sliced
- 1 tbs of chilli paste
- 1 teaspoon of oil
- 1 teaspoon of soy sauce
- 1 tbs of oyster sauce

Direction

- Heat oil, add chili paste, stir fry until fragrant
- Add egg, scramble until done
- Add mushrooms, stir fry until soft
- Add rice, soy sauce spring onion, soy sauce
- Keep stirring until all rice is coated by soy sauce and oyster sauce

58. My Favorite Far East Fried Rice Recipe

Serving: 6 | Prep: | Cook: 5mins | Ready in:

Ingredients

- 2 TB fish sauce
- 1 1/2 TB rice vinegar
- 2 TB sugar
- 2 1/2 TB olive oil
- 2 eggs, beaten
- 1 bunch green onions, trimmed and thinly sliced
- 2 TB minced garlic
- 1 TSP dried red chili pepper flakes
- 2 large carrots, peeled and coarsely shredded
- 2 cups bean sprouts, trimmed if necessary (or shredded zucchini)
- 5 cups day-old jasmine rice, clumps broken up
- 1/4 cup chopped mint or cilantro or basil (or all 3)

Direction

- Combine the fish sauce, rice vinegar and sugar in a small bowl, set aside.
- In a wok or large skillet, heat the oil over medium-high heat. Add the eggs and stir-fry until scrambled.
- Add the green onions, garlic, and pepper flakes and continue to stir-fry for 15 seconds or until fragrant.
- Add the carrots and bean sprouts (zucchini); stir-fry until the carrots begin to soften, about 2 minutes.
- Add the rice and cook for 2-3 minutes or until heated through.
- Stir in the fish sauce mixture and add the fried rice, tossing until evenly coated.
- To serve, garnish the dish with the fresh herbs.

59. Nasi Goreng Indonesian Fried Rice Recipe

Serving: 6 | Prep: | Cook: 25mins | Ready in:

Ingredients

- 2 cups (500 g) long-grain rice, washed in 2 changes of cold water, drained
- 2 1/2 cups (600 ml) cold water
- 3 tbsp peanut oil
- 3 shallots or 1 small onion, very finely chopped
- 1-3 large fresh red chilies, seeded and cut into thin rounds, or 1/2 tsp chili powder
- 1 tsp chopped fresh ginger
- 2 medium carrots, finely diced
- 2 oz (60 g) cabbage, finely shredded
- 1/4 lb (125 g) button mushrooms, quartered
- 1 tsp paprika
- 2 tsp tomato paste or tomato ketchup
- 1 tbsp light soy sauce
- salt, to taste
- For the garnish:
- 1/2 cucumber sliced
- 2 tbsp. Crisp-fried onions
- few sprigs of watercress

Direction

- Place the drained rice and cold water in a large pan. Bring to a boil, uncovered, then simmer for 10-12 minutes, until all the water is absorbed.
- Stir once with a wooden spoon, then reduce the heat to low. Cover the pan and let cook undisturbed for 10-12 minutes. Remove the pan from the heat and set it, still covered, on a wet dish towel. Let stand for 5 minutes.
- Spoon the rice into a bowl, cover with a damp dish towel, and let stand for 2-3 hours, or until cold.
- Heat the oil in a wok. Add the shallots or onion, the fresh chilies or chili powder, and the ginger and stir-fry for 1-2 minutes. Add the carrots and cabbage and stir-fry 2 minutes longer.

- Add all the remaining ingredients, except the rice and garnishes, and stir-fry for 6 minutes, or until all the vegetables are cooked through.
- Add the cold rice and mix it thoroughly with the vegetables over low heat, until it is heated through and takes on the reddish tinge of the paprika and tomato paste. Do not allow the rice to burn. Transfer the mixture to a heated serving dish and arrange the garnishes on top and around the dish.

60. Oven Fried Rice Recipe

Serving: 12 | Prep: | Cook: 60mins | Ready in:

Ingredients

- 2 cups long grain rice, uncooked
- 1 1/2 oz onion soup mix (1 pkg)
- 1/2 vegetable oil - I quite often use only 1/4 cup oil but the taste is better with the 1/2 cup
- 1/4 cup soy sauce - low sodium if you can find it
- boiling water
- 10 oz can sliced mushrooms
- 3 green onions, chopped

Direction

- Pour the rice into a 2-quart greased casserole or 9x13" pan.
- In a large bowl or 4-cup measuring cup, combine the onion soup, oil and soy sauce. Add enough boiling water to make 4 cups.
- Pour the liquid over the rice, add the drained mushrooms and green onions and stir lightly with a fork.
- Cover and bake at 350 for 1 hour.
- (It cooks faster in the 9x13" pan so check earlier)

61. PORK FRIED RICE Recipe

Serving: 6 | Prep: | Cook: 15mins | Ready in:

Ingredients

- 1/2 CUP orange juice
- 1/3 CUP LOWER SODIUM soy sauce
- 1TBS light brown sugar
- 1 TBS cornstarch
- 1/4 TSP salt
- 2 pork loin RIB CHOPS, 1 LB, BONED AND SLICED
- 2TBS oil
- 2 eggs BEATEN
- 2 cloves garlic, THINLY SLICED
- 1 RED OR green pepper, SLICED
- 3 CUPS COLD cooked rice
- 1 head broccoli, FLORETS,\ TRIMMED, STEMS PEELED AND SLICED, 6 CUPS

Direction

- WHISK TOGETHER ORANGE JUICE, SOY SAUCE, SUGAR, CORNSTARCH AND SALT. TOSS 2 TBS SPOONS JUICE MIXTURE WITH PORK; RESERVE HEAT1 TBS OIL IN LARGE NONSTICK SKILLET OVER MEDIUM HIGH HEAT. ADD EGGS; COOK, STIRRING, UNTIL JUST COOKED THROUGH, 3-4 MINUTES.
- IN SAME SKILLET, HEAT REMAINING 1 TBS OIL OVER MEDIUMHIGH HEAT. ADD GARLIC AND PEPPER; COOK STIRING, 3 MINUTES. ADD RICE. SPREAD IN SKILLET; COOK 1 MINUTE; STIR, SCRAPING RICE FROM BOTTOMOF SKILLET, UNTIL BROWNED.
- STIR BROCCOLI, AND REMAINING JUICE MIXTURE. COVER; COOK UNTILBROCCOLI IS TENDER, 5 MINUTES. STIR IN EGGS AND PORK MIXTURE. HEAT THROUGH; 2 MINUTES

62. Paella Style Fried Rice Recipe

Serving: 4 | Prep: | Cook: 30mins | Ready in:

Ingredients

- 1 tbsp vegetable oil
- 2 small chorizo sausages, cut into slices
- 1 onion, sliced
- 1 garlic clove, chopped
- 1 tbsp turmeric
- 600g cooked plain rice
- 200g frozen cooked prawns
- 100g frozen peas
- lemon wedges, to serve

Direction

- Heat oil in a frying pan.
- Tip in the chorizo, onion and garlic, then cook for a couple of mins until softened.
- Stir in the turmeric
- Then add rice, prawns and peas and 150ml boiling water.
- Keep stirring until everything is warmed through and the water has been absorbed.
- Serve with lemon wedges.

63. Papa Oning's "Sinalamog" Fried Rice Recipe

Serving: 5 | Prep: | Cook: 12mins | Ready in:

Ingredients

- pork lard (left-over adobo lard can be used)
- 1 egg, beaten
- 5 tbsps of chopped garlic
- about 8 cups of left-over steamed rice (the night before making this dish, put the leftover rice in the freezer for better results)
- salt to taste

Direction

- Before cooking this dish, mix the egg and rice together.
- Pre-heat your wok on your stove for about 3 minutes on high heat
- Add the pork lard.
- Sauté the chopped garlic until just before it turns golden brown.
- Add the rice.
- Fry the rice until rice grains separate from each other (or until rice reaches your preferred texture).
- Serve hot with breakfast viand of choice.

64. Pauls Chicken Fried Rice Recipe

Serving: 4 | Prep: | Cook: 20mins | Ready in:

Ingredients

- 4 tablespoons vegetable oil
- 1 egg
- 8 ounces boneless skinned chicken breast, sliced into strips
- 1/2 bell pepper, chopped
- 1/2 cup onion, chopped
- 1 cup bean sprouts
- 3 cups cooked, cold brown rice
- 2 tablespoons light soy sauce
- 1 tablespoon rice-wine vinegar
- salt to taste
- black pepper to taste
- red pepper to taste

Direction

- Lightly beat egg in a small bowl.
- Heat wok or skillet up with 1 tablespoon oil and fry egg into a thin sheet. Remove to plate and reserve.
- Heat wok or large non-stick skillet over medium high heat. Add 2 tbsp. oil. Add chicken, red pepper, and green onion. Cook 5 minutes until chicken is cooked through.

- Add bean sprouts. Stir and cook 2 minutes. Meanwhile combine soy sauce and rice vinegar in a small bowl.
- Add remaining tbsp. oil in skillet. Add cold rice and stir well. Cook for one minute. Add the soy sauce and rice vinegar. Season with salt and pepper, dusting across the surface of the rice. Add Red pepper to taste. None for mild, a little for medium, or several teaspoons for hot. Reduce heat to medium.
- Take your turner and break up clumps of rice as finely as possible to ensure that the sauce is absorbed. Keep stir-frying until all rice is broken up and heated through.
- Shut heat off. Cut up sheet of egg into small pieces and stir into rice, or remove rice to serving platter and garnish with egg slivers.
- Note: Cold, leftover rice is best for this recipe. Feel free to experiment and substitute your favourite veggies such as mushrooms, peas, etc. You can also use white rice.

65. Peruvian Fried Rice Recipe

Serving: 8 | Prep: | Cook: 27mins | Ready in:

Ingredients

- 2 1/5 lbs rice
- 1 lb 10 oz pork
- 12 garlic gloves (3 T ground)
- 2 onions, chopped
- 2 tomatoes, peeled, seeded, chopped
- 4 Aji chillies, seeded, deviened, washed , ground
- 6 T shortening
- 1 T oregano
- 4 T cilantro
- 1 1/2 C peas (optional)
- 1 1/2 C cabbage leaves julienne (optional)

Direction

- Cut pork meat in small pieces (1.5 inches / 3 cm). Place shortening in pan, fry pork until golden. Reserve meat.
- Fry garlic, chili, onions and tomatoes in same fat. Add oregano and cilantro.
- Add reserved pork meat and cover with hot water. Bring to a boil and cook until meat is tender. Incorporate peas and cabbage. Season.
- Add rice, stir and cover with boiling water. When mixture starts to boil, lower heat and continue cooking until rice is done.

66. Peruvian Style Fried Rice Recipe

Serving: 6 | Prep: | Cook: 10mins | Ready in:

Ingredients

- cooking spray
- 2 larg eggs, beaten
- 3 Tbs. toasted sesame oil
- 1 lb. medium shrimp, peeled and deveined
- 2 cups (8oz.) chorizo, chopped
- 1 onion, cut into 1/2" pieces
- 4 cups cooked white rice, cooled
- 1/4 cup soy sauce
- 2 Tbs. sherry
- chopped cilantro, for garnish

Direction

- Heat a medium, non-stick skillet over high heat and coat with non-stick spray. Pour half of the eggs into the pan, swirling to coat the bottom, and let cook until set, about 1 minute.
- Remove the skillet from the heat, flip the eggs and cook for 1 minute more.
- Transfer the egg "tortilla" to a cutting board and repeat the process with the cooking spray and remaining egg. Roll up each egg "tortilla" and slice cross-wise into 1/4" thick strips.
- In a large skillet, heat the sesame oil over high heat. Add the shrimp, chorizo and onion and

cook, stirring, until the shrimp is just opaque, 1 to 2 minutes.
- Mix in the rice, soy sauce and sherry. Cook until heated through. Stir in the egg strips and garnish with cilantro.

67. Pinapple Shimp Fried Rice Recipe

Serving: 4 | Prep: | Cook: 25mins | Ready in:

Ingredients

- 1 lb Shimp peeled and divined
- 5 eggs
- 5 sliced sweet pinapple (can be from a can)
- 1/2 cup of frozen peas and carrot mix
- 1 green onion- scallion chopped
- 4 tbsp of light soy sauce or kikoman sauce
- 2 tbsp of fish sauce
- pinch of msg (optional)
- 3 glove garlic crushed

Direction

- In a large skillet, add oil and garlic cook until golden brown.
- Add frozen peas and carrot, cook until access water.
- Add egg, cook until it little hard and crispy. Make a little spot in middle of the skillet, add shrimp and cook until pink.
- Add rice and light soy sauce, fish sauce, green onion, msg and pineapple, stir to mix.
- Arrange on serving plate or in a fresh pineapple boat. ENJOY!!

68. Pineapple "fried" Rice Recipe

Serving: 4 | Prep: | Cook: 25mins | Ready in:

Ingredients

- cooking spray
- 2 eggs, whisked in a bowl with s+p to taste
- 1-2 tbsp vegetable oil (I used Canola)
- 1 cup chopped onion
- 2 garlic cloves, minced
- pinch crushed red pepper (or to taste)
- 1 cup chopped carrots
- 1 cup button mushrooms, quartered
- 1 cup snow peas, trimmed & halved
- 1 cup mung bean sprouts, roughly chopped
- 2 cups cooked rice (I used Basmati) - leftover 1-2 days is best
- 1 cup chopped pineapple
- sesame oil, to taste
- soy sauce, to taste
- rice vinegar, to taste
- ground sea salt & black pepper, to taste
- 1 green onion, trimmed & sliced thinly on an angle

Direction

- Prepare a small skillet with cooking spray. Heat over medium. Add eggs and cook until set, about 2-3 minutes. Flip and cook another 1 minute, or until done through. Set on cutting board to cool. Once cool, roll up and slice in thin strips.
- Heat veg oil in a large skillet over medium-high heat. Add onions and cook for about 5 minutes, stirring occasionally. Add garlic and crushed red pepper. Cook 1-2 minutes, stirring occasionally.
- Add carrots and cook 2 minutes, stirring occasionally. Add mushrooms, peas, and sprouts. Cook about another 3 minutes, stirring occasionally, until peas are tender crisp.
- Add rice, egg, and pineapple. Season with sesame oil, soy sauce, rice vinegar, and a bit of s&p (less is more to start). Mix to incorporate, cook to heat through - about 3-5 minutes. Add more seasoning if needed.
- Garnish with sliced green onion to serve.

69. Pineapple Fried Rice Recipe

Serving: 8 | Prep: | Cook: 20mins | Ready in:

Ingredients

- 1/4 cup cooking oil
- 3 eggs slightly beaten
- 1 tablespoon chopped garlic
- 2 Chinese sausages diced
- 1/3 cup dried shrimp soaked for 20 minutes and drained
- 1/2 cup sliced white onions
- 4 cups cooked rice
- 1/2 pineapple diced to 1/2"
- 1 tablespoon fish sauce
- 2 tablespoons soy sauce
- 2 chopped red chilies
- 1 green onion chopped
- tomato slices
- cucumber slices

Direction

- Heat wok over high heat then when hot add 2 tablespoons of the oil.
- Add eggs and cook 30 seconds then add garlic, sausage, shrimp and onion and cook 1 minute.
- Add remaining oil and rice then cook 3 minutes then add fish sauce and soy sauce.
- Stir in pineapple and mix well about 2 minutes then sprinkle with red chilies and green onion.
- Garnish with tomato and cucumber slices.

70. Pineapple Fried Rice Recipe

Serving: 4 | Prep: | Cook: 5mins | Ready in:

Ingredients

- 8 rings canned pineapple
- 1/2 carrot/1 red pepper
- 1/2 onion
- 1 green onion
- 1-2 tbs jalapeño pepper
- 1 tsp minced garlic
- 1 tsp minced ginger
- 2 cups cold rice(I like scented) (1-2 day old rice is the best
- 2 tbs soy sauce
- 1 tsp curry powder
- 1 tsp sugar(optional)

Direction

- Grate carrot
- Wash and chop pepper
- Peel and chop onion
- Finely chop green onion
- Heat oil
- When it is hot:
- Add garlic and ginger cook 30 seconds
- Add onion cook for 1 minute
- Add pepper/ carrot and pineapple
- Add rice stir about 2 minutes or until rice is shiny
- Add soy, curry and sugar
- Stir and serve

71. Pineapple Thai Fried Rice Recipe

Serving: 46 | Prep: | Cook: 12mins | Ready in:

Ingredients

- 1/3 cup dried shrimp
- 2 tablespoons vegetable oil
- 1 tablespoon minced garlic
- 2 (2 ounces each) Chinese sausages, cut diagonally into 1/4-inch slices
- 1/2 cup sliced onion
- 3 eggs, lightly beaten
- 4 cups cold cooked long-grain rice
- 2 tablespoons soy sauce
- 1 tablespoon fish sauce
- 1 cup diced fresh pineapple
- 1/2 pineapple, hollowed out, for serving

- 1 tomato, cut into 1/4-inch thick slices, for garnish
- 1 small cucumber, cut into 1/4-inch thick slices, for garnish
- 1 to 2 teaspoons thinly sliced fresh thai chile, for garnish

Direction

- Soak dried shrimp in warm water to cover until softened, about 20 minutes; drain.
- Place a wide nonstick frying pan over high heat until hot. Add oil, swirling to coat sides. Add garlic and cook, stirring, until fragrant, about 10 seconds. Add dried shrimp, sausages and onion; stir-fry for 1 minute. Add eggs and stir-fry for 30 seconds.
- Decrease heat to medium; stir in rice, separating grains with the back of a spoon. Cook for 2 minutes. Add soy sauce, fish sauce, and pineapple. Cook, stirring, until heated through.
- To serve, spoon fried rice into pineapple shell and garnish with tomato, cucumber, chile, and green onion. Or place tomato and cucumber slices around the edge of a serving platter, place fried rice into the middle of the platter, and sprinkle with chile and green onion.

72. Pork Fried Rice Recipe

Serving: 8 | Prep: | Cook: 20mins | Ready in:

Ingredients

- 1 onion
- 1 pkg bacon
- 8 eggs
- 2 boilin bags of rice
- soy sauce
- pinch of salt/ pepper

Direction

- Cook bacon till crisp put to side to cool
- Dice onion and sauté in a little of the bacon grease
- Scramble eggs and cook with onions
- Cook rice to directions on box then add to eggs/onions
- Crumble bacon and add to rice, eggs and onions
- Add soy sauce to taste along with salt and pepper
- Mix and heat up for a few more minutes

73. Proper Fried Rice Takeaway Style Recipe

Serving: 2 | Prep: | Cook: 10mins | Ready in:

Ingredients

- 500 grams of cooked basmati rice.
- 2 tablespoons of oil, not olive oil.
- 2 medium eggs.
- 2 Tablespoons dark soy sauce.
- 1 Tablespoon light soy sauce.
- 1 teaspoon of table salt.
- 1 teaspoon of white pepper.
- 1 teaspoon of oyster sauce.
- 1/2 teaspoon of msg (optional)
- Few drops of good quality toasted sesame oil

Direction

- Firstly the soy sauces must be good quality no supermarket rubbish. I order my essentials from wing yip (UK based)
- Looking at the ingredients you can see how simple it is too make. However you must realize that cooking any Chinese dish on a home cooker will never give you the smoky effect called wok hei, you would get on a good outdoor burner or what they use in takeaways/restaurants
- I use an Eastman wok burner for professional results.
- Pre-cooked rice.

- I would always recommend using a rice cooker to boil your rice as it gives the best start to fried rice. Always rinse your rice a few times in cold water before you boil it. This ensures the starch content has been removed otherwise you end up with sticky rice.
- Once cooked leave the rice to cool completely. You do not leave it overnight in the fridge. In my experience this makes the rice hard and clump together.
- Fried rice.
- Crack both eggs into a cup and beat together then set aside.
- Heat up your wok to medium, adding 2 tablespoons of oil.
- Once slight smoking add the egg and continuously mix the egg into a scrambled egg effect.
- Turn the heat to highest possible.
- Add the cooked rice and press the rice flat (TOP TIP... use a ladle), toss the rice and egg and flatten the rice once more with the back of the ladle.
- Add the dark soy sauce and stir fry for 2 minutes, keep flattening the rice.
- Add the salt and pepper and stir fry for one more minute, keep flattening the rice.
- Add the light soy sauce and oyster sauce, stir frying for two minutes, keep flattening the rice.
- Add the MSG if you wish and stir fry for 3 minutes, keep flattening the rice.
- Add the sesame oil, toss ingredients for 30 seconds and serve.
- Easy!!
- TOP TIP... The rice is ready when you hear it popping and slight charred. By the end step if your rice is still wet keep stir frying for a few minutes longer until the grains are loose and no longer wet.

74. Quick And Easy Fried Rice Recipe

Serving: 4 | Prep: | Cook: 6mins | Ready in:

Ingredients

- 1 Tablespoon canola oil
- 1 package confetti vegetable mix from Walmart (chopped broccoli, cauliflower, radish & cabbage)
- 1 package Uncle Ben's 2 minute long grain rice
- Quick & Easy Asian Sauce (separate recipe)

Direction

- Heat canola oil on medium heat until clear
- Add confetti vegetable mix and cook on medium heat until begins to soften (1-2 minutes)
- Add package Uncle Ben's 2 minute Long grain rice
- Add Quick & Easy Asian Sauce and cook another 4 minutes (stirring somewhat often) until everything is heated thoroughly and veggies are at desired tenderness.

75. Red Curry Fried Rice Recipe

Serving: 4 | Prep: | Cook: 25mins | Ready in:

Ingredients

- 1/2 lb shimp peeled and devined
- 1/2 cup of pork or beef ball cut into 4 pieces
- 1 tbsp of red curry pasted (see my red curry recipes)
- 3-4 tbsp fish sauce or to taste
- 2 lime leaves thinly sliced (optional)
- 2 fresh red chili pepper (optional)
- celantro leave for garnish
- pinch msg (optional)
- 3 tbsp of oil
- 2 tbsp of green onion chopped
- 3 cup of cooked jasmine rice

Direction

- In a large bowl, removed cooked rice and set aside
- In a large skillet, add oil, lime leaves and red curry pasted cook about 5 minutes in low heat for fragrant.
- Add meat ball and shrimp, cook until shrimp are pink.
- Add cooked rice and fish sauce, msg, green onion and red chili pepper if desire.
- Stir well to mix.
- When done, place fried rice on serving plate and top with cilantro leaves and it ready to serve...ENOY!!!

76. Red Fried Rice Recipe

Serving: 2 | Prep: | Cook: 30mins | Ready in:

Ingredients

- 2 plates of rice
- 100 gr of shrimp
- 100 gr chicken
- 1 egg
- salt
- 1 tbl spoon sweet soy sauce
- 1 tbl spoon ketchup
- 1 tbl spoon oyster sauce
- oil
- ====================
- spice:
- 3 cloves garlic, blend with
- 5 shallots

Direction

- Pour the oil into the pan, heat it. Put the egg, and fry it, make a scramble egg. Take them up
- Add the oil into the pan, after it was heat up, sauté the spice, until its fragrance appear. Then put the shrimp and the chicken, stir until it done.
- Put the rice and egg, finely stir, then add salt, soy sauce, ketchup and oyster sauce. Stir it until it's all mix together, and finely done.

77. Rice And Corn Recipe

Serving: 8 | Prep: | Cook: 15mins | Ready in:

Ingredients

- 2 cups white jasmine rice
- 6-8 cloves of fresh garlic (chopped)
- 1 teaspoon salt (I use see salt)
- 2.5 cups water
- 1/2 cup frozen corn or more up to 3/4 cup
- 1Tablespoon oil

Direction

- Put the 1 tablespoon of oil to heat up in a medium size pot, when it is hot add the chopped garlic. Let it brown, once it is light brown add the rice and fry it for a bit make sure you stir it so that it has oil all over. Add the salt and water. Let it boil, Cook it at a high temperature 6 or 7 on the electric stove, once it boils turn the heat down to temperature 2. When you see the water has been absorbed by the rice, add the corn and mix it. Let it cook for 15-20 more minutes, and that's it!
- Enjoy

78. Salted Fish Rice Recipe

Serving: 0 | Prep: | Cook: 15mins | Ready in:

Ingredients

- 4 tablespoons vegetable or peanut oil
- 4 cloves garlic, minced
- 1 medium onion, minced
- 1/4 cup dried fish fried then shredded
- 2 tablespoons rice wine (optional)

- 6 cups cooked white rice, cooled
- 1/2 teaspoon salt
- 1/4 teaspoon white pepper
- 2 eggs, cooked scrambled then chopped
- chopped spring onions
- olive oil

Direction

1. Mince onions and garlic. Set aside.
2. In a pan, scramble eggs and fry using olive oil.
3. Chop the scrambled eggs.
4. In a separate pan, heat 4 tablespoons of oil. Sauté garlic and onions until fragrant.
5. Add dried fish and fry until cooked.
6. Add rice wine and cooked rice; mix together then season with salt and pepper.
7. Add chopped eggs and mix well. Remove from heat and sprinkle with chopped spring onions.

79. Sausage Or Spam Fried Rice Recipe

Serving: 4 | Prep: | Cook: 10mins | Ready in:

Ingredients

- 2 tablespoons oil
- 1 inch piece ginger, chopped
- 3 cloves garlic, chopped
- 3 Thai green chillies, chopped(optional)
- 1 small yellow onion, sliced
- 2 green onions, tops and stems separated and sliced diagonally
- 4 Oscar Meyer weiners or 1 can Spam
- 1 large bunch baby bok choy, leaves and stems separated and sliced
- 1 tablespoon dark soy sauce
- 1 tablespoon oyster sauce
- 3 tablespoons light soy sauce
- 3 cups rice cooked and cooled(I used half white and half brown)
- 10 medium white mushrooms, sliced
- 1 tablespoon toasted sesame oil

Direction

1. Heat oil in a wok and fry the ginger and garlic until it starts to get fragrant.
2. Add the green chilies, yellow onion, and white part of the green onion and fry until the onions get translucent.
3. Now add the wieners or Spam and fry until the meat gets a little browned.
4. Add the stems of the bok choy along with oyster sauce and both the soy sauces and mix well.
5. Add the rice and mix well so it is coated all over by the sauce and breaks up any lumps of rice.
6. Add the mushrooms and the tops of the green onions and the leaves of the bok choy and fry for 1 min until evenly mixed into the rice.
7. Now put in the sesame seed oil and turn off the stove before mixing it well into the rice.
8. Serve hot.

80. Sauteed Rice With Cumin Seeds Mustard Seeds Onions Curry Leaves Green Chilli Coriander Turmeric Recipe

Serving: 2 | Prep: | Cook: 15mins | Ready in:

Ingredients

- Onion medium diced
- Cumin seeds half table spooon
- Mustard seeds half table spoon
- Turmeric 1/4 table spoon
- Oil 2 table spoons
- Salt as per taste
- Curry leaves 10 to 15
- Coriander half table spoon
- Green chilli 1-2

- Cooked rice half cup

Direction

- Get your pan in high heat pour the oil
- In with your mustard and cumin, let them splutter
- One they splutter put the onions in (this will stop them seeds all over your kitchen counter)
- Next up turmeric. Sauté in oil till you get nice aroma bit don't. Burn
- Next Curry leaves and green chili (cut horizontally) go in
- Sautéed them
- First add salt and then Rice goes in .mix rice well to infuse the turmeric and all other spices
- Add coriander finely chopped to rice and mix it well
- Leave this on stove for about 10 mins on low flame for. Rice to absorb all the flavours
- Plate up and enjoy

81. Scallop Fried Rice Recipe

Serving: 2 | Prep: | Cook: 20mins | Ready in:

Ingredients

- 5 scallops
- 4 stalks of kai lan - thick stems only
- 1 clove garlic, smashed
- 4-5 cups cooked rice
- 1 egg white
- 1 heaped tbsp of dried mini anchovies
- 1 stalk green onions (spring onions), chopped
- white pepper to taste
- salt
- pepper
- cornflour

Direction

- Wash scallops and pat dry so that you can sear properly or moisture will cause scallops to steam. Season scallops lightly with salt, pepper and corn flour.
- Heat up 2 tbsp. vegetable oil in wok. Medium heat. When oil is hot enough, use tongs to transfer scallops to wok. Sear scallops for 3-5 minutes on each side or until they turn golden brown. Set aside.
- Cut kai lan stems (at their cross section) into small pieces. Add kai lan pieces and smashed garlic to wok and allow to cook for about 2 minutes. Set aside kai lan, leaving garlic in the wok.
- Add cooked rice to wok and use spatula to mix the rice with the tasty brown bits left in the wok by the scallops.
- Make a small "well" in the center of the wok. Add egg white and mix well with rice. Add dried mini anchovies and mix well.
- Cut scallops into quarters. Transfer scallops, kai lan and green onions to wok. Add a few dashes of white pepper. Mix well and serve.

82. Shiitake "Fried" Rice Recipe

Serving: 4 | Prep: | Cook: 25mins | Ready in:

Ingredients

- 1 cup basmati rice (may use brown rice)
- 1 tbsp vegetable oil
- non-stick cooking spray
- 2 large eggs, beaten
- 3.5 oz. shiitake mushrooms, stems removed & sliced thin
- 2 garlic cloves, minced or grated
- crushed red pepper flakes to taste
- salt & pepper to taste
- 3 tbsp lime juice, freshly squeezed if possible
- 2 tbsp soy sauce
- 2 scallions, green & white parts sliced thin

Direction

- Cook rice according to directions on package (I used 1tbsp butter with mine).

- Spray medium skillet & heat over medium. Add egg, season with salt and pepper. Cook 2-3 minutes, until set. Flip and cook for about another minute. Transfer to a cutting board and let cool. Once cool, roll up and slice in thin strips.
- Add oil to skillet. Once heated, add mushrooms and cook for 2-4 minutes until tender - stirring often. Add garlic and red pepper flakes, salt & cook for another minute. Then, add cooked egg, rice, soy sauce and lime juice. Mix thoroughly. If rice has cooled since cooking, make sure heated thoroughly. Top with scallions & serve.

83. Shrimp Fried Rice Recipe

Serving: 6 | Prep: | Cook: 5mins | Ready in:

Ingredients

- 2 tablespoons fat-free, less-sodium chicken broth
- 2 tablespoons rice wine or sake
- 1 tablespoon low-sodium soy sauce
- 1 teaspoon dark sesame oil
- 1/2 teaspoon salt
- 1/4 teaspoon freshly ground black pepper
- 2 tablespoons vegetable oil
- 2 large eggs, lightly beaten
- 2 cups chopped green onions
- 1 tablespoon minced peeled fresh ginger
- 5 cups cooked long-grain rice, chilled
- 1 pound medium shrimp, cooked, peeled, and coarsely chopped
- 1 (10-ounce) package frozen green peas, thawed

Direction

- Combine first 6 ingredients in a bowl; set aside.
- Heat vegetable oil in a wok or large non-stick skillet over medium-high heat. Add eggs; stir-fry 30 seconds or until soft-scrambled. Add onions and ginger; stir-fry 1 minute. Add rice, shrimp, and peas; stir-fry 3 minutes or until thoroughly heated. Add broth mixture; toss gently to coat.

84. Simple Fried Rice Recipe

Serving: 4 | Prep: | Cook: 30mins | Ready in:

Ingredients

- 1 cup rice
- 2 cups water
- 1 cup mixed veggies
- 1 egg
- 1/4 cup soy sauce or to taste
- 1 section fresh garlic
- 1tbsp butter

Direction

- In a med pan, add rice and water and boil until tender, set aside.
- In a large frying pan, cook egg, place egg in bowl to side.
- Crush garlic and fry in pan until golden brown with tbsp. butter.
- Add rice and veggies in pan; Mix well on med heat stirring frequently as to not burn the rice.
- Add egg and soy sauce, mix and serve!
- ** You can also add Chives, onions, or bell peppers**

85. Simple Indian Fried Rice Recipe

Serving: 3 | Prep: | Cook: 6mins | Ready in:

Ingredients

- 1 large bowl - cooked boiled rice (leftover from previous cooking)
- 1 large onion chopped
- 2 green chilies chopped in button shape

- 1 tsp mustard seed
- 1 tsp Urad Dal (split black gram without skin)
- 1 tbsp curry leaves
- 2 tbsp "ghee" (Indian style heated butter) or refined oil
- salt to taste

Direction

- Put "kadai" (Indian style deep frying pan) on stove at medium flame
- When the kadai heats up, pour ghee
- When some fumes start appearing add mustard seed
- When the mustard seeds starts crackling, add "urad dal"
- When urad dal starts becoming a little darker, add chopped onion & chilies
- About after 15 second, add curry leaves
- When onions become transparent, add rice
- Fry well so that rice does not stick to bottom, add salt
- Keep frying the mix till all ingredients are well mixed
- Serve hot with veg salad and potato chips (optional)

86. Simple Yummy Fried Rice Recipe

Serving: 4 | Prep: | Cook: 45mins | Ready in:

Ingredients

- cooked jasmine rice, black sesame seeds, butter, garlic salt, some herb if you like

Direction

- Prepare a 2 cups of rice, you may take 20 mins to cook with a rice cooker (may also use old rice about a day old)
- When rice is done leave the rice cooker uncovered for about 15 mins
- Prepare a wok and wait till it heats up and put 2 table spoons of butter in the wok make sure it has all melted.
- Put in the rice and stir well make sure most of the rice has some touch of butter on it sit for about 5 min on a mid-high stove
- Put it one tea spoon of garlic salt and stir well
- Lastly sprinkle some ground herb and black sesame seeds.
- Enjoy!

87. Soy Free Chicken Fried Rice Recipe

Serving: 4 | Prep: | Cook: 30mins | Ready in:

Ingredients

- 2 chicken breasts
- 4 cups brown Minute Rice
- 4 cups chicken broth
- 2 teaspoons butter
- 1 carrot
- 1 celery stalk
- 1/2 white onion
- 1/4 red pepper
- 1/4 yellow pepper
- 1/4 green pepper
- 1 can mini corn cobs
- 1 egg
- 1 tablespoon cooking oil
- salt, pepper, dry parsley, dry chicken broth seasoning

Direction

- Combine minute rice, chicken broth and butter in microwavable dish. Cover and cook on high power 18 minutes. Let stand, then fluff with a fork.
- Cut all veggies and chicken into tiny pieces.
- Heat oil in a pan. Add chicken. Sauté while seasoning with salt, pepper, and dry chicken broth seasoning. Remove cooked chicken from the pan

- Cook the egg in the same pan. Separate it into small pieces. Then add veggies. Season again, and add the chicken.
- Throw in the rice. Cook until hot and enjoy!!!

88. Spanish Fried Rice Recipe

Serving: 6 | Prep: | Cook: 30mins | Ready in:

Ingredients

- 1 cup of uncooked white rice
- olive oil
- 1 to 2 shallots finely chopped
- 1 to 2 minced garlic cloves
- 1 medium to large chopped onion
- 2 deseeded finely chopped jalapeno peppers
- salt and pepper to taste
- 1 teaspoon cumin or to taste
- 1 cup of chicken broth
- 1 cup of tomatoe sauce OR 1 cup of diced tomatoes with juice, depending on personal taste.

Direction

- Coat the bottom of a cast iron skillet with olive oil, bring to medium heat.
- Add the uncooked white rice
- Toast the rice until it turns slightly brown to brown, stirring occasionally
- Once the rice is toasted add the shallot, onion, garlic. Continue to cook ingredients 3 to 4 mins longer.
- Pour in the chicken broth, tomato sauce, jalapeno peppers, salt, pepper and cumin. Stir ingredients thoroughly.
- Cover and let simmer about 20 or 30 mins until rice is done and free of liquid.
- Serve hot, I personally like to refrigerate and serve warm the next day.

89. Spicy Chicken Fried Rice Recipe

Serving: 2 | Prep: | Cook: 20mins | Ready in:

Ingredients

- diced onions
- Crushed garlic
- Ground white pepper
- ground ginger or galangal
- 2 Tablespoons of light soy sauce
- 1 tablespoon of dark soy sauce
- 3 tablespoons of peanut oil
- chicken thighs sliced into cubes or strips
- salt and black pepper (to taste)
- Red finger peppers (or chili flakes)
- frozen vegetable mix
- One sprig shopped cilantro
- 2 jumbo eggs
- One cup cooked steamed rice, cooled overnight in the fridge

Direction

- Marinate the chicken with the light soy sauce and white pepper and let sit for 10 - 15 minutes.
- Heat a large wok over high heat and add 2 tablespoons of the peanut oil. Swirl to coat the wok.
- Add the onions, garlic, and red peppers and toss briefly, allowing the onions to cook till soft (approx. 2-3 minutes).
- Add the chicken and stir fry for about 5 minutes, and then reduce the heat to medium and let the chicken sit for another two minutes to cook through.
- Now it's time to fry your eggs. Remove the food from the wok and add the remaining one tablespoon of oil. Swirl to coat the wok. Crack your eggs into the wok and scramble them lightly with a bamboo spatula.
- Add the chicken back in along with the frozen vegetable mix and toss for a couple of minutes. Turn the heat back up to high, add the cooled rice and dark soy sauce and toss together until

food is distributed evenly throughout the rice. Allow about 5 minutes total time for all the food to warm (by this step, each of the ingredients is cooked so it's just a matter of warming the food).
- Season with salt and pepper to taste. Divide into two portions and garnish with cilantro.

90. Stir Fried Rice Recipe

Serving: 8 | Prep: | Cook: 40mins | Ready in:

Ingredients

- 3 cups rice
- 6 cups water
- ½ tsp salt
- ¼ cup oil
- ½ cup green onions
- 2 cloves garlic pressed, through garlic press
- ½ cup soy sauce
- ½ cup frozen peas and carrots
- 3 eggs, beaten well

Direction

- Place rice, water and salt in rice cooker or large pot with a tight fitting lid. If using rice cooker, allow to cook normally. If using a large pot, bring to a rapid boil, stir once, put lid on and cook over low heat for 20 minutes.
- Allow rice to cool completely.
- Heat oil in large frying pan. Stir fry green onions and garlic, being careful not to burn the garlic.
- Add rice (break it up with your hands as you add it to the frying pan) and stir rice until it has all had a chance to cook in the hot oil.
- Add the soy sauce and frozen peas and carrots (this is my preference, you can use any type of vegetable or cooked meat that you like).
- Stir well, reduce heat, put a lid on it and cook, stirring a couple times, about 10 minutes.
- Pour egg into hot rice. I like to drizzle it all through it, allow to cook one or two minutes,

and stir once more before removing from heat and serving. Some prefer to make a well in the middle of the rice, let the egg cook and then stir into the rice.

91. Szechuan Orange Chicken Fried Rice Recipe

Serving: 0 | Prep: | Cook: 17mins | Ready in:

Ingredients

- 1 ½ cups orange juice
- ½ cup sugar
- 1 tablespoon minced fresh ginger
- 1 ½ tsp minced garlic
- ½ tsp hot chili flakes
- 1 lb boneless skinless chicken breast cut into ½ inch chunks
- 4 cups cold cooked rice(break up lumps and crumble with your fingers)
- vegetable oil
- ¼ cup thinly sliced spring onions (reserve some for garnishing)
- 3 tbsp soy sauce

Direction

- To make Orange Sauce, mix all sauce ingredients in a non-stick skillet over high heat.
- Bring to boil and boil until reduced to 1 cup, about 10 minutes. Stir often to prevent burning.
- Heat oil in a wok or a skillet. Add chicken and stir-fry until lightly browned and cooked through for about 4-5 minutes.
- Add Orange Sauce and stir until it comes to a boil for about 1-2 minutes.
- Mix in the rice, soy sauce and spring onions for another couple of minutes.
- Garnish with more spring onions.
- Serve hot!

92. Tea Fried Rice Recipe

Serving: 2 | Prep: | Cook: 20mins | Ready in:

Ingredients

- 1 tbl sake or rice wine
- 1/4 c tamari sauce or soy sauce
- 1 tbl green tea liquid
- 1 tsp sesame oil
- 1 tbl mirin
- 1 tsp vinegar
- 1/2 tsp minced ginger
- 1/4 c frozen or fresh peas
- 2 tbl brewed green tea leaves (I use genmai cha)
- 2 scallions chopped fine
- 2 tbl veg oil
- 2 cups cooked rice (day old is the best)
- 1 beaten egg (jumbo) or 2 small

Direction

- Mix first 7 ingredients well
- Heat veggie oil over a medium heat and toss in the peas, stir a minute especially if they are frozen.
- Add the tea leaves, stir.
- Add scallions and stir fry for about a minute
- Next add the rice and break it up in the pan
- Pour the tamari mixture over the rice and stir the liquid in well
- Stir fry and mix well until the liquid is absorbed and the flavors marry
- In a separate pan cook beaten egg
- When the egg is done fold it into a triangle and serve in the same bowl with the rice.
- Top with a little tamari, soy or salt if you wish.
- Great for breakfast or anytime!

93. Thai Fried Rice Recipe

Serving: 2 | Prep: | Cook: 5mins | Ready in:

Ingredients

- 2 portions of steamed thai rice
- 1 fried chicken, shredded
- 1 egg
- 3 tbs olive oil
- 2 cloves of garlic, minced
- 2 hot chilli peppers, finely sliced
- 1 tbs of Thai red curry paste
- 1 tbs of thai soy sauce
- 2 tbs of thai oyster sauce
- pinch of salt and pepper
- finely sliced scallion

Direction

- Sautee garlic, chili and oil in low heat, until fragrant
- Add egg, turn into high heat, and add chicken
- Add Thai red curry sauce, rice, soy sauce, oyster sauce, salt, pepper, and scallion, mix well, serve hot

94. Thai Red Curry Fried Rice Recipe

Serving: 2 | Prep: | Cook: 15mins | Ready in:

Ingredients

- 5 Cups Steamed white rice
- 8 oz. Diced chicken breast
- 2 cloves garlic, Minced
- 1/2 Cup basil leaves
- 1 Cup Diced red bell pepper
- 2 Thai chili peppers, Chopped
- 2 Medium eggs
- 2 Tbsp. vegetable or canola oil
- 1 1/2 Tbsp. red curry paste (Mae Ploy Brand)
- 2 Tbsp. fish sauce
- 2 Tbsp. soy sauce
- 1 lime wedge (optional)

Direction

- In a bowl, beat 2 medium eggs. Fry in skillet on medium with just a little bit of oil and set aside.
- Crank up the heat to medium high and pour rest of oil in skillet, adding chicken breast, red curry paste, garlic, basil, red peppers, and chopped chili peppers and fry for about 4-5 minutes.
- Add 5 cups steamed white rice into the stir fry, pouring fish sauce and soy sauce over the rice. Stir fry for another 5 minutes, making sure the red curry paste coats the rice and turns it into a reddish color.
- Before turning off the heat, add the cooked eggs and mix it well into the fried rice.
- Garnish with 1 lime wedge.

95. Thai Shrimp Fried Rice With Pineapple Recipe

Serving: 0 | Prep: | Cook: 15mins | Ready in:

Ingredients

- 4 cups cold cooked rice (break up lumps and crumble with your fingers)
- vegetable oil
- 1 tbsp garlic, coarsely chopped
- ½ cup shallots, chopped
- ½ lb medium shrimp, peeled and deveined
- 2 tbsp fish sauce
- ½ tsp sugar
- 1 can pineapple chunks, drained
- 2 tbsp spring onions, thinly sliced
- 2 tbsp fresh cilantro, chopped

Direction

- Heat oil in a wok, and then add garlic and shallots and toss well until shiny and fragrant for about 1 minute.
- Then add shrimp and cook, tossing until the onion begins to wilt and shrimp are pink and cooked through for about 2-3 minutes.
- Add rice, fish sauce, and sugar and toss well.

- Add pineapple and spring onion and cook about 2 min more, tossing often, until rice is tender and heated through.
- Garnish with cilantro.
- Serve hot!

96. Tomato Fried Rice Recipe

Serving: 1 | Prep: | Cook: 10mins | Ready in:

Ingredients

- 1 serving of cooked white rice, refrigerated for at least an hour or overnight*
- 1/4 bell pepper, cut to small pieces
- 4 white/brown button mushrooms, sliced
- 1 hot dog, sliced
- 2 tbsp tomato sauce/ketchup (preferably Japanese type)
- 1 tbsp olive oil
- 1 tbsp chopped garlic
- 1/2 tbsp chopped basil/basil flakes
- 1/2 tbsp chopped onion
- 1 egg (optional)
- a small pinch of salt (optional)
- 1 chilli padi, cut to small pieces (optional)
- * Note: Purpose of using refrigerated rice is to prevent them from sticking during frying - tip I learnt from VideoJug

Direction

- Heat oil in wok. Sauté garlic, onion, chili & basil till fragrant.
- Add bell peppers & mushrooms and stir fry for a minute.
- Add hotdog, salt and rice. Try to break the rice apart gently using a wok turner.
- When the rice is separated, add the tomato sauce and stir fry until evenly mixed and dry.
- If you wish, you can cook an egg separately and garnish on top of rice. Enjoy!

97. Tuna Fried Rice Recipe

Serving: 3 | Prep: | Cook: 15mins | Ready in:

Ingredients

- 1 can 5 oz chunk tuna
- 2 - 3 cups mixed vegetables (corn, carrots, peas, beans)
- 1 1/2 cups rice
- onion (chopped)
- 2 cloves garlic (minced)
- pickled capers (optional)
- olive oil
- 1 tsp Maggie Magic Sarap (optional)
- salt
- pepper
- feta cheese

Direction

- Cook 1 1/2 cups of rice. Set aside.
- Drain the liquid in the can of tuna.
- Heat pan and put olive oil.
- Put onion and garlic.
- Once garlic is lightly brown and onion is transparent, add the mixed vegetables. Cook for 5 mins.
- Then add the tuna. Cook for a couple of minutes.
- Add the cooked steamed rice. Mixed well.
- Then add the Maggie Magic Sarap and capers.
- Taste and season with salt and pepper if necessary.
- Serve hot. Top with feta cheese. (^_^)

98. Vegetable Fried Rice Recipe

Serving: 6 | Prep: | Cook: 15mins | Ready in:

Ingredients

- vegetable Fried rice
- 1-tbspn sesame oil
- 2-tspn bottled minced garlic
- 2-tspn fresh minced ginger
- 1-cup jarred red peppers, chopped
- 1 green bell pepper, chopped
- 1-onion chopped
- 1 small can sliced mushrooms, drained
- 1-cup baby carrots, sliced lengthwise three times each carrot
- 1 head of bok choy coarsely chopped
- 3=cups cooked brown rice, cooled
- 1 green onion, snipped tops and bottom

Direction

- Cook garlic and ginger in oil for 1 ½-minutes.
- Add mixed vegetables and bok choy and cook for 8 minutes.
- Stir occasionally.
- Add rice and soy sauce and cook and stir for about 5 minutes. Sprinkle with green onions and serve.

99. Vegetarian Fried Rice Recipe

Serving: 4 | Prep: | Cook: 15mins | Ready in:

Ingredients

- 5 eggs, beaten
- 1 T cooking oil
- oil as needed
- 1 medium onion, chopped
- 1 clove garlic, minced
- 2 stalks celery, thinly bias-sliced
- 4 oz fresh mushrooms, sliced
- 1 medium green sweet pepper, chopped
- 4 c cold cooked rice
- 1 - 8 oz can bamboo shoots, drained (optional)
- 2 medium carrots, shredded
- 3/4 c frozen peas, thawed
- 3 T soy sauce or more to taste
- 3 green onions, sliced

Direction

- The stir-fry secret is a hot pan.

- Gather all ingredients, utensils and serving bowl before you start, this is a quick process.
- Make sure pan is hot before each stir-fry.
- Add oil to pan after each stir-fry.
- Mix veggies after each addition to serving bowl.
- In a small bowl break eggs and add 1 tablespoon water, set aside.
- Put 1 tablespoon cooking oil into a wok or heavy skillet.
- Preheat over high heat.
- Stir-fry chopped onion and garlic in hot oil about 2 minutes or until, onion is wilted; remove to serving bowl.
- Add egg mixture to wok and scramble until set; remove eggs from the wok to serving bowl. Chop up large pieces of egg.
- Stir-fry celery in hot oil for 1 minute; remove to serving bowl.
- Add mushrooms and sweet pepper to wok; stir-fry for 1 to 2 minutes more or until vegetables are crisp-tender. You may want to rinse your pan, dry and add more before adding the rice.
- Add cooked rice, bamboo shoots, carrots, and peas to wok.
- Cook and stir until heated.
- Make a well in center of pan and put 3 tablespoons soy sauce in the center.
- When the soy sauce foams, start blending in the rice mixture to pick up the flavor (this prevents the rice from being wet with the sauce; repeat if more sauce if needed).
- Add to serving bowl and add green onions and mix well.
- Serve immediately.
- Garnish with lemon slices and tomatoes, if desired.

100. Vietnamese Fried Rice Recipe

Serving: 68 | Prep: | Cook: 165mins | Ready in:

Ingredients

- 2 bunches scallions
- 3 large carrots
- 2 cups fresh bean sprouts
- 2 large eggs
- For seasoning Liquid:
- 3 tbs Asian fish sauce (any oriental store carries this)
- 1 1/2 tbs rice vinegar (no substitute)
- 2 tbs sugar
- Other:
- 5 cups chilled Chinese white rice
- 1 1/2 tbs corn or safflower oil
- 2 tbs minced garlic
- 1 tsp dried hot red pepper flakes
- 1/4 cup chopped fresh cilantro or mint leaves
- 1/2 cup chopped dry-roasted peanuts

Direction

- Finely chop enough scallions to measure about 2 cups and coarsely shred enough carrots to measure about 2 cups. Rinse bean sprouts and trim stringy root ends. In a small bowl, lightly beat eggs.
- Make Seasoning Liquid:
- In a small bowl, stir together seasoning liquid ingredients.
- In a deep 12 inch heavy nonstick skillet heat oil over moderately high heat until hot but not smoking and stir fry eggs until scrambled, about 30 seconds. Add scallions, garlic and red pepper flakes and stir fry about 15 seconds or until fragrant. Add carrots and bean sprouts and stir fry until carrots begin to soften, about 1 minute. Add rice and cook, stirring frequently, 2 to 3 minutes, or until heated through. Stir seasoning liquid and add to fried rice, tossing to coat evenly.
- Serve fried rice sprinkled with cilantro or mint and dry roasted peanuts.
- Serves 4 as a main dish or 6 to 8 as a side dish.
- Chinese Rice:
- 2 3/4 cup long grain Chinese rice
- 4 cups water

- Put rice in a 3 to 4 quart heavy saucepan and, using your fingers as a rake, rinse under cold running water. Drain rice in a colander.
- In a pan, bring 4 cups of water to a boil with rice. Simmer rice, covered, over moderately low to low heat until steam holes appear on surface and water is absorbed, about 16 minutes.
- With a fork, fluff rice and spread in a shallow baking pan. Cool rice completely.
- Chill rice, covered with plastic wrap, at least 12 hours. Rice may be made 2 days ahead and chilled in a sealable plastic bag.
- Makes about 10 cups.

101. Wild Rice Stir Fried Recipe

Serving: 4 | Prep: | Cook: 20mins | Ready in:

Ingredients

- 2 cups chicken broth
- 1 cup wild rice
- 1/4 cup sesame oil
- 1/2 cup chopped bok choy
- 1 tablespoon chopped garlic
- 1 tablespoon chopped fresh ginger
- 1/4 cup julienned red bell pepper
- 1/4 cup diced poblano chili
- 1/4 cup bean sprouts
- 1/4 cup scallions chopped
- 2 tablespoons hoisin sauce
- 2 tablespoons chopped fresh cilantro
- 1 teaspoon fresh lime juice

Direction

- In a medium saucepan over medium low heat combine the chicken broth and wild rice.
- Cover and cook for 20 minutes.
- Remove from heat and let stand for 10 minutes.
- In a wok over high heat warm the sesame oil.
- When hot add the bok choy and stir fry for 15 seconds.
- Add the garlic and ginger and stir fry for 15 seconds.
- Stir in the bell pepper, poblano chili, bean sprouts and scallions then stir in the wild rice.
- Add the hoisin sauce, cilantro and lime juice and stir to mix.
- Serve immediately.

102. Yang Chow Fried Rice Recipe

Serving: 4 | Prep: | Cook: 15mins | Ready in:

Ingredients

- 6 cups cooked leftover jasmine rice (overnight in fridge is better) or use any leftover rice with grains well separated.
- 3/4 cup shrimps, shelled and deveined
- 3/4 cup honeycured ham, cubed
- 3 eggs, beaten, scrambled and chopped
- 1 cup frozen peas and carrots
- 2 stalks green onion, minced
- 2 cloves garlic, minced
- 1 scallion, minced
- 1 tsp kosher salt
- freshly ground black pepper
- 1/2 tsp cornstarch
- 2 tbsp cooking oil
- 1 tbsp soy sauce
- 1 tsp sesame oil

Direction

- Marinate shrimp with salt, pepper and cornstarch for 10 mins.
- Heat a large wok and add oil. Swirl to coat entire pan.
- Sauté garlic and scallions.
- Add shrimp and ham cubes. Stir.
- Add carrots and peas. Stir.

- Add rice, green onions, scrambled eggs and sesame oil.
- Move ingredients around, don't let anything stick to the sides and bottom of pan. Using a Teflon-coated or non-stick wok is better.
- Season with salt and pepper. Drizzle with soy sauce and toss.
- Serve HOT.

103. Yangchow Fried Rice Recipe

Serving: 4 | Prep: | Cook: 20mins | Ready in:

Ingredients

- 3 large eggs
- 6 ounces roast pork diced
- 4 ounces frozen medium shrimp
- 1/2 teaspoon salt
- 1/2 teaspoon freshly ground black pepper
- 1/2 teaspoon cornstarch
- 5 tablespoons oil
- 1 medium yellow onion diced
- 1/2 cup frozen peas thawed
- 4 cups cold cooked rice

Direction

- Lightly beat the eggs and set aside then dice the barbecued pork.
- Rinse shrimp under warm running water to thaw then shell devein and finely chop.
- Toss shrimp with the salt, pepper and cornstarch.
- Heat wok and add 1 tablespoon oil.
- When oil is hot add shrimp and stir fry until they turn pink.
- Push the shrimp up to the side and add the roast pork.
- Stir fry briefly then remove both from the pan and set aside.
- Clean out the pan then heat wok and add 2 tablespoons oil.
- When oil is hot add onion then stir fry until it begins to soften then add the peas.
- Stir fry until the peas turn bright green and remove from the pan.
- Heat 2 tablespoons oil in the wok then add cooked rice stirring to separate the individual grains.
- Do not let the rice brown then add beaten egg stirring so that all the rice grains are covered.
- Add pork, shrimp, onion and vegetables into the pan then mix everything together.
- Taste and season with extra salt and pepper if desired then serve hot.

104. Chinese Shrimp Fried Rice Recipe

Serving: 2 | Prep: | Cook: 5mins | Ready in:

Ingredients

- 3 bowls of cooked rice (cold)
- 100 grams of shrimp
- 2 eggs
- 1/2 bowl of finely sliced spring onion
- 1 garlic, minced
- 1 chilli, roughly chopped (if you like the heat)
- 2 tbs of soy sauce
- pinch of salt
- pinch of white pepper
- pinch of sugar or hon dashi (to replace msg)

Direction

- Heat your wok, sauté garlic and chilli until fragrant
- Add shrimp, stir until shrimp turns pink, add eggs, and stir
- Add rice, add soy sauce, salt, pepper, and sugar/hondashi
- Toss well, add spring onions, toss to mix everything well, serve

105. Chinese Fried Rice Recipe

Serving: 2 | Prep: | Cook: 5mins | Ready in:

Ingredients

- 2 eggs
- 2 portions of cooked rice
- 1 tbs of minced garlic
- 1/2 teaspoon of minced garlic
- 1 finely sliced chilli pepper (optional)
- 3 tbs of soy sauce
- 1 tbs of oyster sauce
- pinch of salt and pepper
- 1 cup of finely sliced scallion

Direction

- In low heat sauté garlic, chili and ginger until soft and fragrant
- Add egg, scramble until done
- Add rice, keep stirring
- Add soy sauce, oyster sauce pepper and salt
- Make sure you mix everything well, every grain of rice has to be coated with soy sauce, taste
- Add scallion, mix again, serve hot

106. Korean Kimchi Fried Rice Recipe

Serving: 2 | Prep: | Cook: 5mins | Ready in:

Ingredients

- 1 cup of kimchi, drained, chopped
- 2 cups of steamed rice
- 2 tbs sesame oil
- 1 teaspoon of korean chilli paste
- 1 teaspoon of korean paprika powder
- salt and pepper to taste

Direction

- Sauté kimchi until fragrant
- Add paprika powder, rice, the rest of the ingredients
- Stir well, taste, serve hot

107. Malaysian Fried Rice Recipe

Serving: 5 | Prep: | Cook: 10mins | Ready in:

Ingredients

- rice
- anchovies(i prefer the small ones)
- bird chillies
- onion
- eggs
- dry chilly paste
- sliced cucumber

Direction

- Heat the oil. Add the onion.
- Add in the chili paste. Fry until cooked.
- Add in the bird chilies if used.
- Add in anchovies.
- Fried until anchovies are cooked.
- Add in the eggs.
- Wait until cooked.
- Add in the rice.
- Mix well.
- Serve with sliced cucumber.

108. Quick Fried Rice Recipe

Serving: 4 | Prep: | Cook: 15mins | Ready in:

Ingredients

- 3 cups of leftover cooked rice(you dont need that much, but thts what we normally have)
- 2 tsp minced garlic

- 2tsp minced ginger
- 1 thai chilli(can you tell i like hot food?)
- 1/2 onion chopped
- 1 cup frozen mixed vegetables
- 2 large eggs(beaten well till light in color)
- Optional:
- 1 1/2 TBSP dark soy sauce(please read further)
- 3 TBSP oyster sauce

Direction

- Break your leftover rice apart....you should have mostly dry, loose grains of cooked rice
- Heat a wok on high heat and add 1 tsp of vegetable oil (sesame or peanut is good to). Move oil around with your spoon to coat wok nicely
- Add your ginger, garlic, Thai chili, onions and frozen vegetables, and fry for about a minute to brown slightly and remove from wok (just pour it over your rice)
- Add 2 tsp of oil to your wok again and add eggs, let eggs puff up slightly and with your spatula break apart till almost done
- Add your rice and cooked vegetables and stir fry for another 2 minutes till rice it's nice and cooked thru.
- Add salt to your liking and taste preference....
- Optional, after you add the rice, you could stir everything to mix it all up, then add the soy sauce and oyster sauce, and stir fry for about 3 minutes, adding 1tsp of oil to coat the rice nicely. Also please be mindful that dark soy sauce is extremely salty......so reduce as needed according to the rice quantity, the color will come from the oyster sauce.
- Serve piping hot, garnish with green onions or chopped cilantro!

109. Shannons Fried Rice Recipe

Serving: 4 | Prep: | Cook: 10mins |Ready in:

Ingredients

- 4 cups rice warm or cold
- 1 small onion diced
- 4 garlic cloves minced
- 1 tablespoon ginger
- zest and juice of 1 lime
- 2 tablespoons chopped cilantro
- 2 green onions chopped
- i tablespoon rice vinegar
- 1 tablespoon oil

Direction

- Heat oil in wok and cook onion and ginger.
- Now add the garlic, rice, cilantro, zest and juice of the lime and the vinegar. Heat through and add the green onion.
- Serve and enjoy!

110. Thai Seafood And Pork Fried Rice Recipe

Serving: 2 | Prep: | Cook: 10mins |Ready in:

Ingredients

- 2 bowls of cooked rice (cold)
- 50 grams of seafood (shrimp & squid)
- 50 grams of pork (finely sliced)
- 100 grams of kay lan or cabbage
- 2 eggs
- 50 grams of onions, finely sliced
- 2 garlic, finely chopped
- 1 chilli (if you like the heat)
- 1 fresh tomato, cut into smal slices
- 1 tbs soy sauce
- 1 tbs oyster sauce
- 1 teaspoon fish sauce
- pinch of sugar
- 2 tbs of oil
- pinch of salt and pepper

Direction

- With oil, sauté garlic and onion (chili) until fragrant
- Add pork, keep stirring until pork is cooked and brown
- Add seafood, stir well add tomatoes, gai lan toss well
- Add eggs, scramble,
- Add rice, soy sauce, oyster sauce, fish sauce and sugar, salt and pepper
- Taste, if it's not salty enough you can add more fish sauce
- And if you like a richer flavor add more oyster sauce
- Serve hot
- PS: if you like, you can serve it with a sunny side up :)

111. Thai Spicy Fried Rice Recipe

Serving: 2 | Prep: | Cook: 30mins | Ready in:

Ingredients

- dried red chilli pepper 4 or you can put more of how hot you want, smash
- fish sauce / salt / or soy sauce
- thick soy sauce 5 table spoon or as dark you want your rice to be
- lemon 1 cut into wages
- chicken 2 slices breast
- cook rice 2 cups
- green onion / scallion 1 bun, dice into smaill cube
- msg / can be use if needed
- eggs 3 ommelet super hard and crispy
- garlic 3 grove, smash and chop into small pices\
- cucumber / slice

Direction

- Cut chicken into a long slice, put a side
- In small nonstick pan, oil, garlic, and dried pepper cook until it golden brown, put slice chicken in. After chicken is cook put in rice, fish sauce, thick soy sauce, cook eggs, msg and green onion. Stir the rice until well mix and it ready to serve. Garnish with lemon wages and slice cucumber. This dish is best serve hot...

Index

A
Anchovies 3,29
Apple 8

B
Bacon 3,7,20
Beef 3,7,27
Bran 8,45

C
Chicken 3,4,8,9,14,25,32,42,43,44
Chilli 4,39
Chives 41
Coconut 3,10
Coriander 4,39
Crumble 21,36
Cumin 3,39
Curry 3,4,11,37,39,40,45

D
Dal 7,42

E
Egg 3,14,22

F
Fish 3,38

G
Garlic 3,20
Gin 3,11,20,21

H
Ham 3,25

L
Lobster 3,19

M
Mango 3,26
Mince 3,25,27,39,45
Mushroom 3,21,29
Mustard 3,39

O
Oil 39
Onion 4,22,39
Orange 4,44

P
Paella 3,32
Peas 17
Peel 17,22,35
Pepper 3,11,20
Pineapple 3,4,16,34,35,46
Pork 3,4,5,26,36,52
Port 23
Prawn 3,14

R
Rice 1,3,4,5,6,7,8,9,10,11,12,13,14,15,16,17,18,19,20,21,22,23,24,25,26,27,28,29,30,31,32,33,34,35,36,37,38,39,40,41,42,43,44,45,46,47,48,49,50,51,52,53

S
Salt 3,26,38,39
Sardine 3,24
Sausage 3,8,39
Scallop 4,40
Seafood 3,4,15,52
Seasoning 48

Seeds 3,4,39

T

Tea 4,17,45

Tofu 3,19

Tomato 4,46

Turmeric 4,39

V

Vegetarian 4,47

W

White pepper 26

Conclusion

Thank you again for downloading this book!

I hope you enjoyed reading about my book!

If you enjoyed this book, please take the time to share your thoughts and post a review on Amazon. It'd be greatly appreciated!

Write me an honest review about the book – I truly value your opinion and thoughts and I will incorporate them into my next book, which is already underway.

Thank you!

If you have any questions, **feel free to contact at:** author@fetarecipes.com

Marie Chunn

fetarecipes.com

Printed in Great Britain
by Amazon

55180977R00033